THE PROPHETHOOD OF BLACK BELIEVERS

ALSO BY J. DEOTIS ROBERTS AND
PUBLISHED BY WESTMINSTER/JOHN KNOX PRESS

Black Theology in Dialogue

The Prophethood of Black Believers

AN AFRICAN AMERICAN
POLITICAL THEOLOGY
FOR MINISTRY

J. Deotis Roberts

Westminster/John Knox Press
Louisville, Kentucky

Scripture quotations from the New Revised Standard Version of the Bible are copyright © 1989 by the Division of Christian Education of the National Council of the Churches of Christ in the U.S.A., and are used by permission.

Book design by Drew Stevens

Cover design by Frank Perrone

First edition

Published by Westminster/John Knox Press
Louisville, Kentucky
This book is printed on acid-free paper that meets the American National Standards Institute Z39.48 standard. ∞

PRINTED IN THE UNITED STATES OF AMERICA
9 8 7 6 5 4 3

Library of Congress Cataloging-in-Publication Data

Roberts, J. Deotis (James Deotis). date
    The prophethood of Black believers : an African American political theology for ministry / J. Deotis Roberts. — 1st ed.
          p.   cm.
    Includes biographical references and index.
    ISBN 0-664-25488-8 (alk. paper)

    1. Afro-American clergy.   2. Afro-American churches.   3.Afro-Americans—Religious life.   I. Title.
BR563.N4R616   1994
200'.89'96073—dc20   93-32901

FOR MY GRANDCHILDREN:

André, Jazmin, and Jewell

Contents

Introduction

"We are engaged in this ministry."

2 Cor. 4:1

THE SUBJECT OF THIS BOOK HAS CONCERNED ME FOR many years. It has been inspired by my theological reflection and practice of ministry. As a lifelong theological teacher and educator, I have been greatly moved by the way in which my students, past and present, have carried out a dedicated and effective ministry among all sorts and conditions of human beings. In this study, the emphasis will be upon ministry in black churches, but its message will have currency wherever the word is preached and the sacraments are duly administered.

My own ministries have been varied since I was ordained in 1946. I served as pastor in North Carolina, Connecticut, and Scotland. During my formative years I served as minister to migrant workers and students. Also I was privileged to assist outstanding pastors. Among these were Dr. Henry Moore of the Ebenezer Baptist Church in Charlotte, North Carolina, and Dr. J. C. Jackson in Hartford, Connecticut. Such apprenticeships are usual in the black Baptist tradition. Having such able and caring senior mentors gave my ministry a head start.

As a young theologian and campus minister at Shaw University, I also assisted Dr. O. S. Bullock at the First Baptist Church in Raleigh, North Carolina. Even after I was appointed theologian at Howard University Divinity School, Dean Daniel G. Hill gave me the responsibility of supervisor of fieldwork for a few years. This opportunity to relate to students and pastors in Washington and Baltimore was a great blessing to my lifetime ministry. In this role I was able to share experiences. It kept me in touch with ordinary people and allowed me to develop a love for preaching.

My ministry has also included work in prisons, in hospitals, and on military installations, at home and overseas. My larger ministry, however, has been in the education of men and women for ministry. My life has been spent primarily as theologian and in theological education as the dean of Virginia Union's School of Theology and as president of the Interdenominational Theological Center in Atlanta. In 1984 I became a theologian at Eastern Baptist Theological Seminary.

While my devotion to ministry explains my desire to write this book, it is important to mention that I strongly believe in the mission of the church. It is for this reason that my anchor has usually been in the seminary. At times I have taken leave from the seminary for academic involvement, for research, and to serve as a college or university professor. But these have been brief periods of refreshment, reflection, and renewal. The sense of ministry as a divine call has not permitted me to distance myself from the life of the church even during the withdrawals from the seminary. The mission of the church has always been a clear summons for me. It has been obvious for me since ordination that my life should be dedicated to ministry in and through the church. Accordingly, as a theologian also trained in philosophy, I have always considered my role as that of interpreter of the faith for the people of God (Matt. 28:20).

The need for this book has been becoming more clear to me over several years. The development of the doctor of ministry degree created a clear mandate for the subject matter of this book. This advanced professional degree in ministry builds upon the basic pastoral degree, the master of divinity (M.Div.). I was challenged by the seasoned practitioners in ministry who returned to the seminary to think with them about aspects of ministry. Many had discovered their gifts in certain aspects of ministry. They desired to prepare themselves for a more effective witness in some other aspect of ministry. They needed a theological updating as well as serious theological reflection on their ministry. In lectures and discussion we attempted to empower their resources for ministry. Their needs and questions were different from the beginners in ministry.

In the black church tradition there is another group of ministers for whom this book is written. There are many gifted and able pastors who for one reason or another were not privileged to obtain a formal theological education. These men and women are involved in a dedicated ministry. They require a continuing educational program to inform and empower them for the church vocation.

Whereas in past years many theological students came to seminary early in life, today many have responded to a sense of call to ministry in middle life. These people are often professionals in some nonreligious area of service. They now desire the biblical and theological grounding for ministry. They have acquired a vast amount of knowledge and experience that can be useful in ministry. The task is to educate these persons for effective ministry. Many have already witnessed as lay persons in the church. They now seek the status of ordained minister and leader of a congregation.

In many classroom settings in theological schools we have two age groups in the same classes. In some cases doctor of ministry and master of divinity students share advanced seminars. But even in the master of divinity classes one finds a significant number of people with different life experiences. The rapid increase in the number of women studying for ministry and seeking ordination has further enriched the range of human experiences these seminary students have had. Thus, this situation provides a rich context for peer learning. It challenges the theologian to provide the proper reflection for this rich encounter.

Outside the seminary walls, there is the need for education and renewal for laity and clergy alike for more effective ministry. In the urban context, it is now essential to take the classroom process to churches, community centers, and pastoral/church institutes where the people are. It is good for the theologian to know the setting where ministry is to be carried out. The theologian is also helped by being in touch with people in their life struggles and concerns. This is being done most effectively in Latin America. Some theologians are priests working among the poor and in base communities.

The reader will observe the ecumenical character of this study. Although I am an ordained Baptist minister, my experience as a theologian and minister has not been circumscribed. As a theologian, I have taught for most of my career in ecumenical seminaries. Even now, I teach ecumenically and serve frequently at other denominational seminaries as adjunct professor. My church experience as preacher and lecturer has been in the context of the global Christian community. From my seminary student days I have been involved in ecumenical relations. From the outset, black church studies and black theology have been ecumenical. Hence, all of my experience has brought an ecumenical outlook to this study.

The reader will also note the interdisciplinary character of this study. My theological perspective has grown in relation to several academic disciplines. It began with philosophy and biblical studies. It now includes world religions, ethics, literature, and the social sciences, among other fields of investigation. This broad excursion into various fields of knowledge is useful in reflection upon the African American religious heritage, which is holistic. The secular and the sacred, the personal and the social, the abstract and the practical interface.

The cross-cultural character of this study is also evident. Concern for the centrality of the African heritage and the black experience do not, for me, neutralize what I have learned through vigorous study of the Western religious thought tradition. I have stated very forthrightly my method of theological dialogue in *Black Theology in Dialogue:* "Theology must be particular but not provincial. We need to combine a concrete contextual orientation with a universal vision. Contextualization should lead to humanization for ourselves and the entire human family."[1]

As I reflect here upon ministry in the black church, I will draw upon sources and experiences from the world community. I affirm what seems to be of worth in all cultures and thought-systems. My task remains to understand better the mission and ministry of the black church tradition.

Now, let us turn to a brief overview of what the reader may expect to find in this book.

Chapter 1 begins with a discussion of the ministry of Jesus. The nature and ministry of the church as well as our personal ministries must be based upon a solid understanding of the ministry of Jesus. Through reflection upon the nature of the ministry of Jesus, we find various characteristics that we see as normative for those who minister in his name. The ministry of Jesus is said to be holistic—that is, priestly and prophetic at the same time. We view the church as a corporate extension of the incarnation. Just as the ministry of Jesus was to heal and set free the oppressed, the servant church must also do the same.

Chapter 2 treats ministry in the black church tradition. I view the church in black history as a crucial survival institution, along with the family and the school. The church however, has a spiritual foundation and a redeeming mission. Throughout more than two centuries the black church has been involved in healing the scars of oppression and embattled in vigorous protest against oppression based upon race. The ministry of black churches has been among the oppressed. It is against this background that theological reflection is set forth. What we say theologically about the ministry of black churches must be anchored in this historic setting to be fully meaningful.

Chapter 3 sets the stage for the more detailed discussion to follow. So much has been said in Protestant circles about the priesthood of all believers that I seized upon this concept as a clue for the distinctive ministry described in this study. The "priesthood of believers" indicates that the church is the people rather than the priests. "Priestly," here, refers to the healing, comforting dimensions of the gospel and the ministry that flows from it. While this is a vital part of the gospel, we need to emphasize the protest content of the mission and ministry of black churches. I describe this as the "prophetic" nature of the gospel. Gayraud Wilmore described this "radicalism" in his classic study.[2] In this chapter we reflect upon "the prophethood of black believers," with a focus on a ministry to the oppressed.

Chapter 4 takes up the black church's involvement in education. Black churches have a great opportunity to shape the thoughts of congregants. They should take this task seriously. Beginning with the pastor as educator, black churches should become teaching churches. Even the study of the Bible should be undertaken with a focus on the formation of Christian character and social uplift for a downtrodden people. Black churches have a unique opportunity to teach moral and spiritual values, especially to the young.

While chapter 4 lays a foundation for an understanding of the teaching mission of the church, chapter 5 focuses upon the task of youth development. In this chapter I emphasize nurture as a process for youth development. The role of the family is central to the message in this chapter, in which I apply much of the insight discussed in an earlier work on the black church and family, *Roots of a Black Future*.[3] We must recognize the different social circumstances from which black youth come and attempt to provide helpful programmatic suggestions for ministry to youth. This is a vital ministry since the future of our people and the nation is at stake in its success.

In chapter 6 we move to pastoral care in black churches. The important studies by Edward Wimberly provide a base for theological reflection in this area of ministry. I touch on pastoral care in the black church tradition, on the way that knowledge and skills in this field of study are brought together with the wisdom of the black church tradition. Against this background we reflect upon the spiral of violence in black communities and the shepherding role of the black pastor and congregation. The therapeutic role of the black church's ministry is seen against the backdrop of its mission as an institution of social transformation.

The ministry of black women receives special attention in chapter 7. Because the number of black women with religious vocations is increasing, this concern is now acute. Most of these women seek ordination and vie for a peer status with men in church leadership. The resistance of many black men in ministry has caused a crisis in the black church leadership. The insistence of most of the men that they have a Bible-based authority for the rejection of women for ordained ministry presents issues that must be overcome by sound exegesis and serious theological reflection. While I make no promise to resolve this critical issue, I have given constructive suggestions regarding a positive resolution of this impasse. Black churches need all the able leadership available. If women are inspired by God to minister, who are we to resist this divine plan?

The economic factor is decisive in human affairs—it is true that humans cannot live by bread alone. Neither can they be fulfilled without bread. Chapter 8 tackles the problem of economic means for human fulfillment. I begin with a theological and ethical consideration of economics. Thereafter I attempt to provide a Christian theological perspective on the economic order. In view is a responsible economic order that makes life more human. I then try to contextualize economics in the black experience. The goal is constructive participation of black ministers and churches in the economic uplift of black people as well as others who are oppressed. This is a structural concern that should be addressed by church bodies and not only by individual Christians.

Politics is another area of involvement for black ministers and congregations. Those who minister to a suffering community must face political realities. Chapter 9 takes up this thorny subject. Much of the history of the black church has been political. As a protest body against injustices due to race, black churches have been on the front line seeking the right to vote, full citizenship rights, and full participation in the political process in the United States. This chapter is an attempt to initiate a serious theological reflection on the *how* and *why* of political involvement of the black church and its leadership in social transformation through political thought and action. I seek to bring political realism and the Christian witness together in the mission and ministry of black churches.

The center of black worship is not only preaching but music. Much has been written on preaching by black scholar-pastors and theologians, but music has not been given adequate attention. Worship in the black church empowers worshipers to serve. Chapter 10, therefore, is an exercise in what Jon Michael Spencer calls "theomusicology." I seek to interpret "soul music" or "the black song" with the intention of this entire study behind the effort. The ministry of the black church is empowered by the depth and quality of black music. Black music is characterized by *praise* and *protest*. Here again, in black music the twin attributes of black ministry, priestly and prophetic, are powerfully manifest.

In chapter 11, the final chapter of the book, I provide a summary and critical conclusion. I do not see this study as the end of a process. My intention is much more modest. I believe there needs to be a constant back-and-forth conversation between full-time scholars and those involved in a day-by-day ministry to God's people regarding the challenges to the black church and its ministries. Some of these challenges are ideological, others are cultural, and still others are practical. For example, Afrocentrism and pluralism are very much with us, and multiculturalism promises to be a powerful influence in black communities rather soon. Black theologians and pastors are going to need to prepare to face many familiar and new challenges. There will need to be action and reflection, reflection and action to be faithful to our time-honored and august mission. I close by pointing to an "unfinished agenda" that pulls us into our future. With God's help we can be worthy.

In sum, ministry in the black church tradition is ecumenical and holistic. There is little dispute over differences of doctrine. There are some ugly power struggles, but they are not over the interpretation of scripture or whether to be involved in social justice endeavors. Most often, struggles are contests for personal power, especially for key leadership positions. While these struggles are not to be praised, they are to be understood for what they are. The common struggle against racist oppression has neutralized the passion for conflicts of a different order. The black caucus movement in all major white church bodies brought black ecumenism to global attention in the late '60s. Black churches are not divided over quietism or activism. Black churches are generally united around actions that seek to make life more human for the oppressed. A holistic perspective on the mission and ministry of the church prevents disunity on this basis.

This study is a personal testimony for a commitment and involvement in the ministry and mission of black churches. I sense a need for this study, if only to inspire others to provide their own reflection. Indeed, I urge pastors to share the fruits of their labors with others through similar reflection. I attempt to make a special contribution to theology and ministry in these pages and especially to the oppressed.

Last, but not least, I have indicated some special characteristics of my own outlook regarding the black church tradition. May reflection upon these matters be useful for the practice of ministry in the church of Jesus Christ.

1

Jesus, the Church, and Ministry

ANY DISCUSSION OF THE CHRISTIAN MINISTRY should begin with the ministry of Jesus. Our ministry at its best should mirror the characteristics of the ministry of Jesus to the full extent possible through the assistance of divine grace. It will, therefore, be helpful if we can look at his ministry at close range for a deeper understanding.

The church that Jesus founded is an extension of the incarnation. Jesus is viewed by Christians as God's supreme salvific revelation to humans through fleshly and historical embodiment. The church is the means by which that revelation is manifest in community and throughout history. This being so, the church becomes important as the context of ministry. It is through the church's mission and ministry that God's will is to be done on earth.

In this chapter we will discuss the personal ministry of Jesus during the days of his flesh. At the same time we will seek to outline the nature of the church he founded as the extension of God's saving purpose in our world. To understand Jesus and the church, in relation to ministry, is to lay a solid foundation for an understanding of our ministry in the church of Jesus Christ.

Exploring the Ministry of Jesus

The ministry of Jesus is to be viewed as comprehensive and holistic. Jesus looked at the entire person. He also was concerned with the individual's proper relation to others. This is true of primary relations in families and small groups, in what we might call interpersonal encounters. Jesus, however, had a concern for human welfare that reached beyond the interpersonal to the systemic. His ministry was a public ministry, in that he opposed systems of power that were dehumanizing. While his ministry included the "least of these," he also challenged the "greatest of these" whenever humans were being treated as nonpersons. The ministry of Jesus was personal, social, and public—it was holistic in the most comprehensive sense. Another way of stating this is that the ministry of Jesus was priestly, prophetic, and public.

The priestly aspect of the ministry of Jesus

The role of a priest is to provide comfort and assurance to those who are suffering or in trouble. In Luke 4:18, Jesus includes in what has been considered his commission to ministry the statement: "He hath sent me to heal the brokenhearted" (KJV). More recent versions leave out this crucial phrase because it is omitted by the best Lucan manuscripts.[1] I prefer to include its meaning as we examine the priestly ministry of Jesus.

The meaning of "priestly" here does not relate to the sacrificial functions of the Jewish priesthood. It has to do more with the compassionate concern Jesus had for those whose life he touched. Jesus often "had compassion" (Mark 6:34) as he saw people who were hungry, anxious, or sick. For example, Jesus would no doubt cast his lot today with the homeless. In South Africa, he would rather dwell in Soweto than Johannesburg. His compassion was always manifest, in action as well as feeling. In this sense the ministry of Jesus was priestly ministry.

One active area of ministry in which Jesus demonstrated this priestly aspect was healing. Jesus showed concern for all types of people in all walks of life through his healing ministry. In fact, healing was so characteristic of the ministry of Jesus that he was dismissed or misunderstood by those who expected a different form of ministry from him. It was, however, the very essence of his self-understanding that ministry should be healing in nature. It is significant that the call to ministry includes the phrase: "recovery of sight to the blind" (Luke 4:18).

In our time and language we would want to include the therapeutic dimension of his ministry. Jesus is said to have had compassion on a multitude that he found confused "like sheep without a shepherd" (Mark 6:34). Those who were confused, misguided, and anxious found in Jesus what Tillich has described as the "courage to be."[2]

The ministry of Jesus included all persons who came before him. There was a sense that each and every person, regardless of sex, race, or class, was equally valuable in his presence. If he had an option, it was for the needy. But there is no indication that he accepted sinfulness anywhere. In the crowd he could single out an individual in need of his healing touch. His heart was always filled with compassion. He was the priest par excellence.

The prophetic ministry of Jesus

One of the great theological insights of Dr. Martin Luther King Jr. was to see an unbroken line between the Old Testament prophets of social justice and the ministry of Jesus.[3] Jesus was not only a priest. He was also a prophet.

If we used in this instance the typologies of Richard Niebuhr, we could say that as prophet, Jesus was "against culture." His words and deeds were iconoclastic vis-à-vis both the religious and political establishments. His sense of the righteousness of God applied to more than personal and interpersonal relationships. The full implications of his liberation message will be seen in discussion in the next setion of his "public" ministry.

Theologically, Jesus was obsessed with the "righteousness of God." This has to do with the ethical attributes of God. Jesus came preaching that the kingdom of God is at hand (Mark 1:15). The "kingdom" of which he spoke is equivalent to the "will of God." Thus, to "seek the kingdom" is to seek righteousness (Matt. 6:33).

Jesus was not anti-legal or antinomian in his outlook. He viewed his message in relation to Old Testament Jewish law in terms of "promise and fulfillment." He challenged his hearers to embody in their convictions and life-styles the substance of God's requirements. He distinguished between the *esse* (essence) and the *bene-esse* (nonessentials) of the Law. His concern for morality began with the "motives and dispositions" of the heart. Thus, if the "root" of ethics is God's righteousness, the "fruit" will bear this out. The center of his ethical message rests in the love of God and neighbor.

This is but a brief introduction to the prophetic outlook of the ministry of Jesus. It is fundamental that we understand the ministry of Jesus in this way. His compassion as a priest did not overshadow his judgment as a prophet. His ministry always upheld the righteousness of God in personal and social life.

The public ministry of Jesus

"Public" here refers to the manner in which Jesus engaged the evils inherent in the systems of power in his time and place. Thus, the ministry of Jesus provides a basis for ministry in the public sphere. His "public" ministry is an intensification of his prophetic ministry. When one takes seriously the life and ministry of Jesus, one finds in that ministry the basis for a ministry with a public dimension. Black ministers have assumed this for more than two hundred years in this country. It is not equally clear that this sense of ministry has been substantially anchored in biblical faith. This task is now before all Christians. It is the basis for our reflection here.

Liberation theologies, especially black and Latin American liberation theologies, have greatly contributed to this understanding of the public character of the ministry of Jesus. This has been manifest in two ways: first, in the way these theologies have viewed evil as systemic, and, second, in their christological formulations.

The understanding of evil in its systemic form greatly enhances insights into the devastating effect of the collective impact of sin and evil. The class analysis of Marxist thought has provided an instrument of interpretation for Latin American liberation theologians. Marxism takes both the collective and economic dimensions of the human situation seriously. It therefore uncovers aspects of evil often overlooked by those who focus mainly upon the personal and interpersonal aspects of human life. When Marxism (freed of dogma) becomes a receptacle for the teachings of Jesus, it can be turned to constructive use. Latin American liberation theology has made constructive use of class analysis to expose and treat the "public" aspects of the message and ministry of Jesus. Here I do not recommend an uncritical use of Marxism, but I do lift up what seems to be a constructive contribution to biblical and theological understanding. A Christian critique of any ideology is necessary.

Black theology, in the United States, has also contributed to a profound understanding of collective evil. It has done so independently of Latin American liberation theology. Black theology developed out of the black church tradition in this country. With this different history and context, black theology has developed out of "race analysis." It is not blind to social, economic, and political factors that contribute to humiliation, deprivation, and suffering. Black theology is deeply grounded in the experience of the Christian faith by black people. It takes both popular culture and biblical faith seriously. It attacks racism as a collective or systemic form of evil. The message and ministry of Jesus are essential to the formulation of black theology. Howard Thurman's *Jesus and the Disinherited* is rightly being lifted up as a landmark volume for the black theology tradition.[4] This work has unusual insight into the humanity of Jesus.

These black and liberation theologians converge on two salient points, as we have seen: the collective nature of sin and evil and similar understanding of the message and ministry of Jesus. The two points are interdependent. Thus, these theologies contribute greatly to our present understanding of the task of ministry based upon the public ministry of Jesus.

One of the important emphases of liberation theologies is the focus given to the earthly life of Jesus. This goes against the grain of certain recent theological movements that stress mainly the existential and

The Prophethood of Black Believers

kerygmatic attributes of the ministry of Jesus. A view of Christology that misses the life and witness of Jesus during the "days of his flesh" cannot do justice to the public dimensions of the ministry of Jesus and what this implies insofar as his public ministry is concerned. The statement in the creeds that "he was crucified under Pontius Pilate" sums up the nature of his public ministry. He was done to death by the religious and political establishments because of his opposition to systemic evil.

It is essential that the priestly, prophetic, and public aspects of the ministry of Jesus be seen as one comprehensive description of a holistic ministry. The ministry of Jesus goes beyond our ability to comprehend. We would only claim that at least these aspects of ministry are manifest and fulfilled in this messianic ministry as described in the Gospels. Our ministry cannot be profound and complete unless we take seriously these aspects of the ministry of Jesus and seek to mirror them in our ministry in his name.

The Church as an Extension of the Incarnation

The church is the body that is to carry on the mission and ministry that Jesus established in his own life and witness. We have already introduced the ministry of Jesus and affirmed that it should be the pattern for all ministries in the church. Thus, it is important that we look at the nature of the church in light of our assessment of the ministry of Jesus.

We begin by asserting that the church is properly understood as a continuation of the ministry of Jesus in a community and through history. Yet, because the church is an organization that exists in time, its true character is easily misunderstood. We want to assert that the church is more than an institution. It is first an organism of the Spirit. It is a living body, the means through which Christ continues his saving work in the world.

In our previous discussion on the ministry of Jesus, we stressed the incarnation as foundational. Jesus we understood to be the embodiment, the enfleshment, the inhistorization of the Word of God. Incarnation brings creation and redemption together. Creation and re-creation are part of one divine purpose, to redeem humankind. Jesus as truly God and truly human pulls the two dimensions of our lives together. God hallows creation through the incarnation. Creation is a means through which the greatest redemptive revelation is concretely manifest in human form. Thus, we insist that God's incarnation in Christ Jesus is concrete and real—it is no mere appearance. God reveals God's self concretely, supremely, and fully in the flesh, in time, through the incarnate Lord.

It is with this certainty regarding this real incarnation of God in Christ Jesus that we can meaningfully assert the reality of the church as an extension of the ministry of Jesus Christ. This means that effective ministry can be established on this understanding of the ministry of the founder of the church. Christians, lay as well as ordained, are to carry on the ministry that Jesus initiated through his life, death, and resurrection.

Jesus promised to send the Spirit as strengthener and sustainer of the community of faithful believers. Thus, some attention needs to be given to the presence and power of Spirit in the mission and ministry of the church. The church was established on the foundation laid in the incarnate life. However, it was born at Pentecost, at the outpouring of the Holy Spirit that infiltrated and empowered those gathered in Christ's name.

The Holy Spirit is a person, member of the divine Trinity. The Spirit shares the eternity of the Father and the Son. The Spirit is the creator spirit of the creation, which turned chaos into cosmos at the creation of the world. The Spirit is eternal as are the Father and the Son. The Spirit is present throughout biblical history. The Spirit was with the judges, prophets, and lawgivers of the Old Testament period. The Spirit was manifest at the birth and baptism of Jesus. The Spirit's presence at Pentecost was a special and powerful manifestation of God's work among the believers assembled in Christ's name. It is important always to understand the Holy Spirit in the context of the divine Trinity and especially in relation to the incarnation—the person and work of Christ. Thus, the Spirit has a special place in the establishment of the church and its ongoing work and witness in the world.

This is an appropriate point to introduce the apostolic witness to the faith inherent in the ministry of Jesus. The self-understanding of the apostles was that they were sent forth to carry on the ministry of Jesus in and through the new community that Jesus had founded. Thus, the words and deeds of the early apostles are to be taken seriously until the end of time. Their witness has a certain authority that makes it exemplary, if not absolutely normative. Yet, we must guard against the dangers of literalism and dogmatism, which can render a disservice to the apostles and the church itself. Even so, we need the direction of their witness to keep our sense of mission and ministry on an even keel, or sound footing.

Many of the apostles had been with Jesus. They were eye-witnesses to his words and deeds. They knew the power of the resurrection in their lives and they shared in the Pentecostal event. Paul, who became one of the greatest apostles, came to know Jesus through a powerful conversion experience. He argues his status by asserting that he did not know Jesus in the flesh, but met Jesus through the power of the Spirit. Paul's ministry

The Prophethood of Black Believers

demonstrates a dedicated life. He, therefore, contributed greatly to the intellectual, spiritual, and leadership aspects of the witness of the apostles to the church for all times. Our ministries receive inspiration and profound meaning from the ministries of the early apostles.

As a part of our understanding of the church, we need to reflect upon what we mean by "the communion of saints." When we look at the church as a historical and communal entity, we must consider its temporal sequence and its universal outreach. The church is in a vital sense *in*, if it is not totally *of*, the world. The church, like the life of individual Christians, is "a treasure in an earthen vessel." Thus, we need to attempt to do justice to the manifestation of the church in the world as the "communion of saints" in an earthly sense.

There is also a spiritual sense in which the church is a "communion of saints." It is an invisible entity as well as a visible and temporal one. A host of saints have departed this life, some during our own lifetimes. Our faith is anchored in a faith in the "resurrection of the dead." We firmly believe that those who have died with faith in Christ's resurrection still live. They are also part of a fellowship to which Christians who still live on earth belong. This fellowship is at once temporal and supratemporal. It is in a real sense one fellowship. We believe with John that eternal life begins now for a devout Christian. It begins in conversion, moves forward through sanctification, and flows into consummation. This being so, the communion of saints refers to one comprehensive fellowship of the living and the dead in and through a saving relationship with Christ in the church as both visible and invisible.

The best understanding of ancestor reverence can, I believe, enrich this aspect of church doctrine. I have listened attentively to my African colleagues as Christian theologians. What they have indicated, as well as what I have arrived at independently through study and observation, leads me to conclude that much can be gained by this cross-cultural encounter. The strong African belief in the close relationship between the "living" and the "living dead" indicates that, traditionally, Africans have held an important belief cherished by all believers in Christ.[5] Add to that foundational belief the doctrine of the resurrection, and one has an even richer belief in the community of faith that reaches both into life and beyond death.

All these assumptions require cautious and critical study. It is exciting for me as a black theologian to explore the possibility that such rich input into theological reflection can flow from ancestral roots in African religion and culture. This helps me to understand some beliefs in black folk culture that have been taken up into the black church tradition. Beyond this there is something here that all open-minded theologians may well consider. In some sense we behold here a universal vision of the communion of saints. This helps us to understand more fully a continuity between the living and the dead in the church, visible and invisible.

The Use of Language in Understanding the Church

It is now time to forge a deeper self-understanding of the church. This is not an easy task. It has a great deal to do with language or the use of language. We are treating an entity that has dimensions beyond our present knowledge and experience. While being earthbound in our concepts and limited experience, we speak of an entity that is the extension of the incarnation and the organ of the Spirit, insofar as Christian believers are concerned.

Feminist theologians have challenged the imagery of the male-dominated way of theologizing. In so doing they have struggled with the use of language. Here I will briefly refer to the insights of Sallie McFague and Susan Thistlethwaite, in turn.

McFague asks us to observe the way a small child encounters meaning. For instance, an infant learns the meaning of red by finding the thread of meaning about the color through observing many dissimilar objects (such as red ball, red apple, and red coat). Thus, the author asserts that "seeing" *this* in terms of *that* provides a thread of similarity amid dissimilars. Just as the child constructs a world, so adults also find a means to expand and transform their world through the use of metaphor. She defines metaphor as follows:

> A metaphor is seeing one thing as something else, pretending that "this" is "that" as a way of saying something about it. Thinking metaphorically means spotting a thread of similarity between two dissimilar objects, events, or whatever, one of which is better known than the other, and using the better known one as a way of thinking about the lesser known.[6]

McFague goes on to demonstrate how this use of language develops theologically. She speaks of Jesus as a parable of God. She also asserts that women may rather see God as Friend than as Father. In these ways she seeks to overcome the hegemony of patriarchy in Western theological discourse.

Susan Thistlethwaite helps us even more as she applies metaphor to a contemporary understanding of the church. If we can be led to understand the church's self-understanding we may also arrive at a more profound view of ministry. Ministry is related to the mission of the church.

Thistlethwaite believes that the use of the appropriate metaphor can lead the church to a real insight into its true nature. She writes:

> Metaphor expresses the heuristic power of thought, which moves from the known to the unknown and enables new knowledge to emerge by association. . . . Metaphor creates new reality by introducing a tension of both likeness and unlikeness, which enables the reality of our experience to be reexamined. Metaphor is the way thought moves, it is thought in action. When metaphors lose this tension, there is a loss of power.[7]

This author affirms the power of metaphor as a means to theological discourse. The language of metaphor includes conceptualization but enters theological reflection at a deeper level. Thus, we seek a metaphorical way to interpret the mission of the church and the ministry that should flow from its self-understanding. I have used many images of the church in my work, especially insights from Paul Minear[8] and Avery Dulles.[9] The images I have used most in reference to the black church tradition are "the people of God" and "the family of God." Here with focus on ministry, I prefer to use the "servant" image of the church. Only as the church becomes a servant and the minister takes upon herself or himself the role of one who serves does profound ministry take place. Here one can ground the understanding of church and ministry in the example of the ministry of Jesus, which we have held up as foundational to all genuine efforts of ministry.

When we think of the servant role of the ministry, we may well conceive of the church as a servant church. The nature of the church will determine the nature of its mission and ministry. Jesus indicated that he understood his ministry as that of a servant. This he spells out in graphic terms.

In the Gospel of John, Jesus demonstrates this self-understanding. He washed the disciple's feet as a demonstration of his servant role (13:3–16). Some Christians have interpreted this event in a literal sense, so that footwashing has become an essential part of the celebration of the Lord's Supper. However, the message that Jesus wishes to pass on to us is clear in his words and deeds. He is teaching servanthood. The measure of greatness is serving and not being served. However we carry out this activity, we miss the high point of the witness of Jesus if we do not understand the central place of servanthood in the life, thought, and example of Jesus.

As we observed at the beginning of this chapter, Jesus articulates his own sense of ministry in the passage of scripture read in Nazareth. This passage from Isaiah relates the Old and New Testaments in terms of promise and fulfillment. The idea of a suffering servant is met in full flower in Isaiah 53. Scholars differ as to whether the Servant in the Isaiah passage is a person or a people. The figure does have the possibility of being a "remnant" or a minority representing and atoning for the sins of many. It can also imply one person representing a host of other persons. All of these insights may be tied up with the notion undergirding the theme of messianic hope inherent in Judaism and Jesus, insofar as Jesus's messianic role or consciousness is concerned. Mark seems to capture the substance of Jesus as a servant-minister. After asserting that greatness comes by way of servanthood, Jesus concludes: "For the Son of Man came not to be served, but to serve, and to give his life a ransom for many" (10:45).

It seems reasonable to conclude from all this that, for Jesus, ministry implied taking upon oneself the role of a servant. One who seeks to follow his example must, therefore, put self in the background and through compassion place those in need in the foreground. The needs to be met may be personal or social, spiritual, or material. Servanthood is the mark of direction for genuine ministry in Christ's name. The church of Jesus Christ is thus a servant church.

2

Ministry in the Black Tradition

THIS AUTHOR VIEWS THE BLACK CHURCH AS A PRIMARY institution. One could speak of the family and the school as primary institutions too. The church, however, differs from those earthly institutions in that it was divinely instituted. The spiritual foundations of the church are primary. The church is the house that love built. We have spoken of it already as an extension of the incarnation. It is more than an organization—it is the organ of the Spirit. This is what the church should mean for baptized believers in Christ, and especially for ordained ministers of the gospel as servants of God's word. Ministers have the task of instructing and leading others in a deeper understanding of Christian discipleship. This they are to demonstrate through deeds and not merely through words alone.

For more than two hundred years, the black church has been a formidable force in black life. This chronicle of religious history has been well presented by eminent black writers such as W. E. B. Du Bois, E. Franklin Frazier, Miles Mark Fisher, and Carter G. Woodson,[1] to name some of them. This discussion will use information drawn from several writers on black religion, theology, and the church, such as from the comprehensive and up-to-date historical discussion provided by Gayraud S. Wilmore in his *Black Religion and Black Radicalism*.[2] Ministry in the black churches has been a ministry to an oppressed community. Black people have been caught up in a bid for survival during their entire sojourn in the United States. This struggle continues. We are aware of some breakthroughs in our development. Although I have been helped by certain changes that have provided new opportunities for black Americans, I remain painfully aware of where I came from, the struggles through which I have moved, and the continuing odds to be faced. Most of all we must be aware of the limited number of blacks who have been in a position to receive the benefits of efforts like affirmative action and fair housing. We must not ignore the fact that the plight of the black masses worsens as a few black people gloat over their success. As servants of the word of liberation, ministers of the gospel, and pastors of those who seek survival, we must identify with the "least of these." This is our calling and our destiny.

A Peculiar Ministry

It is often observed that black theologians have been aloof or indifferent to the mission and ministry of black churches. The need for a black pastoral theology is overdue. Yet, it may be that a black theologian as a full-time scholar will not or perhaps cannot write a definitive study on that vital subject. It will need to be written by a pastor-scholar. It will need to be essentially a reflection-action model of theological discourse. Even so, a full-time theologian can contribute to this effort in important ways, provided he or she affirms the church and is active in its ministry. It cannot be done if the theologian is negative toward the church, viewing its failures rather than its potential strengths for service to the oppressed.

James Henry Harris, who is at once a pastor and university professor of philosophy, presents a point of view that is a distinct challenge to black theologians. He correctly sees these theologians as caught in a crossfire between academic discipline and a practical responsibility for the churches. In his judgment, black theologians have decided to opt for academic respectability. The very language they use and the ideas they express are meant to impress the white counterparts rather than the "folk" about whom they write. He writes: "Black theology has apparently been dialoguing with everyone except 'Aunt Jane' and the black preacher. Few ministers and laypeople laboring in the trenches are aware of black theology, and those who are remain somewhat indifferent to its teachings."[3]

This divide has been a source of great personal concern. I am at a loss to explain why black theology has had so little appeal to black church leaders. Some may find the word "black" troublesome, especially if their theological knowledge comes from a conservative denominational source. They may not have struggled with the meaning of "blackness" and all the action, knowledge, and experience poured into this receptacle for a quarter century. Again, if they were educated in a liberal theological tradition, they may also be alienated by any theological insights that step outside of that tradition, which found its best ethical expression in the Social Gospel, Christian realism, and the ministry and message of Martin Luther King Jr.

Harris further suggests that while black theologians strongly rely upon the tradition of freedom and sorrow songs and sermons, they do not seem to have much respect for the modern black church. Harris continues: "Black churches that have succeeded in white-dominated society tend to neglect aspects of black theology that preserve and celebrate African American culture."[4]

This may provide an important clue as to why the communication between black theologians and ministers has thus far misfired. Black theologians are on a quest for "roots"; black ministers are engaged in survival ministries to the oppressed.

Harris also calls attention to the content of the theological core of black theology, as he views it. He uses the doctrine of God as a point of reference. As one whose primary vocation is that of pastor of a black congregation, Harris believes that academic black theology has not made contact with black folk on the problem of God. For the people, God is not a "problem" but a "presence" and "power." The language is my own. What Harris says is that these black folk are not interested in arguments about the existence of God or the nature of God. They are interested in what God has done and can do (or will do) to help with their *peculiar* concerns and problems. Harris sums up:

> Black folk expect the preacher to reassure them of God's power, not to question or doubt it. They expect the pastor to help them cope with joblessness, poverty and discrimination by transforming their despair into hope. Black theology needs to provide the content and method for changing the social, economic and political obstacles for blacks.[5]

What Harris says here is important and will be appropriately considered in this book. In the meantime, we will look briefly at Gayraud Wilmore's response. Harris had said early in his essay that Wilmore and I have referred often to the need for a black pastoral theology but have done little about it. Wilmore's response should be viewed against that background. More importantly, Wilmore shares with me a profound concern for reaching black churches with the vital substance of black theology. Wilmore, in his rejoinder to Harris, said there are two black theologies. Black theologians have been aware of this from the outset. There is an informal black theology rooted in the black church tradition with its African ancestry. There is also a formal, systematic, and academic Black Theology.[6] This is a salient point. These two projects are interdependent even though they may be carried out by different people. This may imply not only collaboration but also a team effort if an adequate black pastoral theology is to be forthcoming. A peculiar ministry may require a special method if we are to interpret adequately ministry in the black church and community.

The Necessity of Black Theology

We have thus far posited the peculiar ministry to black people and the need for a black theology. This theology should be contextual, developed out of the encounter with the ministry of the black church by those who love the church and are devoted to its ministry. It is not to be "ready-made" in some ivory tower and presented to black congregations. Yet it should not be without serious reflection by those who have the knowledge, the skills, and the opportunity of serious scholarship.

James Harris was ambiguous in his claims about black theology. On one hand, Harris insists that black theology needs to be understandable to the black masses. On the other, he says that black theology uses the language of the masses to make plain the feelings, hopes, dreams, experiences, and practices of black folk. Wilmore agrees with Harris that there is an informal "black theology" resulting from the reflection on God out of the condition and in the cultural idiom of black folk. He also notes there is an academic discipline, Black Theology, taught in seminaries.

To some extent, informal "black theology," according to Wilmore, is to be understood in an anthropological sense. He writes:

It has been said that African American Theology began when the first slave wondered about God whose followers kept people in chains while calling them "brothers and sisters." Frederick Douglass was a black theologian in this sense. Most people who think about the faith out of their experience of oppression and in the style and idiom of black Baptist, African Methodist and Pentecostal churches, or other churches influenced by those same traditions, are in this sense black or African American theologians.[7]

On the other hand, according to Wilmore, formal Black Theology (capitalized, like Social Gospel) is a method of investigating, explicating, critiquing, and sometimes systematizing indigenous religious thought. It is taught in theological seminaries. It sometimes recommends strategies for "praxis," as well. It does not come with the "mother's milk." It belongs to the genre of liberation theologies. It boldly attacks oppression and is grounded in a certain method of theologizing. Black Theology specializes in a certain understanding of scripture and history. It is serious and profound intellectual work and it "demands sweat and midnight oil." Black Theology, Wilmore insists, belongs to both academy and church but should not be confused with either.[8]

Wilmore has said well much that I affirm. We both share a real concern for ministry. We are concerned that greater attention be given to Black Theology in black churches. Nevertheless, a clear distinction should be made between black folk theology and serious theological reflection by competent scholars. For the most part, these religious scholars are devoted to the ministry in the church and are active participants in congregational witness. Their role as scholars is also a ministry that can enlighten and empower others who carry on a full-time ministry at the grass-roots level.

We must see the roles of the theologian and pastor as roles with mutual dependence. The theologian needs to be thoroughly attuned to the worship and life of the local church. Insofar as time and energies permit, the theologian should preach, teach, and carry out other forms of ministry in churches. He or she should work with clergy and laity in seminars and denominational gatherings. The theologian may also share with church leadership through special courses in seminaries. Conversely, the wise theologian seeks "echoes from the field." He or she needs to listen to those whose life is devoted to the daily "practice of ministry." The theologian needs to understand ministry through encounter with "all sorts and conditions" of people, all ages and all classes. Only thus may the theologian's reflections on the gospel and affirmations of faith be meaningful in the church's ministry. The real test of our theology is its importance to the ministry and mission of the church.

In spite of this ongoing concern for theology's relevance for ministry, we theologians are frequently challenged by our lack of contact with the masses. Here I can relate a personal example. On Sundays when I am not preaching or worshiping at my home church, I visit former students who are pastors. It has been an unusual affirmation of my work as theological educator and theologian. The ministers and their members have expressed real appreciation. Usually I decline the offer to deliver the sermon. My goal is to observe the total ministry of my former students, including their message on a particular Sunday. On one occasion, the pastor made glowing remarks about my books and teaching. But, when he asked the members to raise their hands if they knew of my writings, only one woman raised her hand. The pastor was sorry he asked the question. This incident was in some sense a judgment upon my ministry, as I understood it. Why, I ask myself, given the abundance of my writing, had I not reached the rank-and-file membership of this church? The pastor was now reading my latest book, but this did not necessarily translate into direct contact with people in the pew. The time has come for theologians to directly encounter lay people and youth. We will not have fulfilled our role as black theologians until we reach the masses.

Rapprochement: Black Theologians and Pastors

Black theology began in church and community. It has since had its main seat in the academy. To the extent that black theology has lost its strong anchor in the black church, it may be said to be uprooted from the source of its life.

While I am gratified to observe the extent to which black theology has gained academic respectability at home and abroad, I am gravely concerned that it has not informed the ministry of more black pastors.

This state of affairs has not been planned by either group. In fact, in our more pensive moments we wonder why the cleavage has occurred. Black theologians have no doubt been in greater demand in learned circles where new thoughts are examined. Usually they have been based in the academy, where the demands on their time and energy may be overwhelming.

At the same time, many black theologians are ordained and move freely among fellow clergy persons, and yet as bearers of new and disturbing ideas, they are not readily welcomed as black theologians. Many black pastors continue to use sources for personal study and instruction of their people that are likely to contribute to the continual enslavement of their charges.

It will be the task of the theologians to overcome this impasse. If we believe that we have a vital message for black churches, we will need to be more aggressive in our approach. We must present our ideas more palatably.

Black theology is not the latest fad. It is a part of black church history in the United States. We have plumbed the depths of black faith and worship by looking into our history. What we have found is a treasure rich in benefits for all black believers. Even our African roots have been discovered and interpreted for the enrichment and empowerment of black people. Our dignity as persons and our integrity as a people have been explicated and incorporated into a vital understanding of the Christian faith. Both the healing and liberating dimensions of the gospel have been examined and set forth.

If we are to move forward, there are a number of steps black theologians need to take:

First, black theologians should be more visible and aggressive in making their work available to ministers and laity alike.

Second, they should seek opportunities to share their knowledge and experience in churches and church assemblies.

Third, they should seek opportunities to discuss seminal research and ideas at the lay level and in words and ideas that can be understood.

Fourth, they should move freely among the people. When possible, they should get to know fellow clergy and exchange views with them.

Fifth, their publications should be targeted to both the professional and the lay levels. For example, some books should be written with average churchgoers in mind.

Sixth, there should be serious exchanges between professional black theologians and scholar-pastors. The latter are able to translate the works of formal theology into practical aspects of ministry. Theologians need their input and should be good listeners as they do their necessary constructive work.

Seventh, there is a place for institutes with workshops on various aspects of ministry where ministers, laity, and theologians may exchange ideas and experiences regarding ministry and mission in black churches. These learning experiences should include broad participation. Though led by church leaders, they should include many lay people who work with people in many capacities.

Interdisciplinary participants in many fields, such as medicine, law, social work, and the social sciences, should be involved. In short, we need to know the human condition and do our action and reflection in view of comprehensive knowledge and experience. Pastors and theologians should seek together the most effective path for a full ministry.

Eighth, denominations need to invite black theologians and other black religious scholars as writers, editors, and literary workshop consultants and leaders. It is critical that insights from the black theology/church movement impact all aspects of urban ministry, especially as it reaches the laity and youth. All denominational publications should reflect the best black religious scholarship.

Ninth, the exchange between pastors and black biblical scholars, ethicists, and ministers—scholars in all disciplines—is needed. Black churches are not taking full advantage of the resources that are available in abundance. This is, of course, a two-way street; black religious scholars need to be dedicated to the church as well as to their subject matter, to their students, and to academic places of employment. There needs to be mutual growth and enrichment.

Tenth, church music workshops need to include persons with a theological and religious education background. We need new information incorporated into our black music. Black religious thought needs to be a part of the music we use in worship in the black church. Music is a powerful medium for getting new ideas accepted into churchly circles where more established ideas prevail with black youth and the masses. Often the message in black music is not sufficiently informed by black theology.

Eleventh, missions and evangelism need the rethinking that has been done in black theology at home and abroad. We need to look at church growth and the expansion and outreach of the black church to the unsaved as well as the redeemed. Revivalism and renewal as well as all aspects of the life of the church can be enriched and empowered by the insights of black theology.

These suggested steps are an affirmative challenge to black theologians and pastors alike to reflect and work together. They need each other, and together they can enrich and empower ministry and mission in and through black congregations.

"The Social Teaching of the Black Churches"

Peter Paris, in *The Social Teaching of the Black Churches*, describes the social thought and activities of major black denominations, mainly Baptists and Methodists. These are the strong, historic black denominations. They differ from their white counterparts less in doctrine and liturgy than they do on social and ethical questions. Why is there this difference? Paris provides a good summary:

> From the beginning of the nation's history up to the present, the black American experience has been characterized by racism—a phenomenon that employs race as a proscriptive principle for denying rights and opportunities, that is, a principle of societal exclusion. The system of hereditary slavery as practiced in the United States for three centuries, best illustrates the absolutization of that principle. Slavery established a societal condition wherein blacks inherited at birth a status which excluded them from all the privileges normally associated with being human. In short, the logic of the system was based on the proposition that blacks were not fully a part of the human race, a view that frequently sought legitimation in both science and religion.[9]

This is a significant statement regarding the strong impact of racism upon Americans, including the life and witness of churches. To understand why blacks established and still maintain strong denominations, one must consider this history of racist oppression. Unfortunately, 125 or more years after slavery, the cause for separation of black denominations continues. While the abolition of slavery marked the end of its absolute status in defining racial relationships, segregation and discrimination have expressed themselves constantly in different yet powerful forms.

During a period reaching back more than two hundred years, blacks have had independent churches. These black institutions represent the earliest black independent movements in the United States. Because of what blacks had witnessed among whites (so-called Christians), both in slavery and through the most cruel forms of discrimination, blacks needed to separate from them. If they were to take Christianity seriously, they needed a different version—"a nonracist appropriation of the Christian message."[10] Paris writes:

> The black churches were destined to become a surrogate world for black people in general. While the larger society sought to victimize blacks, the black churches aimed at socializing their members into creative forms of coping along with the development of imaginative styles of social and political protest, both grounded in a religious hope for an eschatological victory.[11]

Awareness of the "social teachings of black churches" is critical for the interpretation of ministry in black churches. Thus, the contribution of Paris is very important to any theological perspective on such ministry. Studies by Gayraud Wilmore and Eric Lincoln strengthen this outlook.[12] This data is found most profusely in the black Methodist and Baptist denominations. The adequacy of this data needs to be assessed presently, due to the rapid growth of Pentecostalism among blacks.

Differences in theology among white and black Baptists is less important than differences in this focus on social teachings. Understanding the social concerns of black Baptists is the key to understanding how theology develops in the black church tradition. For instance, a study of black Baptists indicates that what sets them apart from other Baptists and what unites them is their social concern.[13] In fact, until the emergence of black theology, little attention had been given to the difference between black Baptists and the predominant white Baptist denominations. Black Baptists of a more liberal outlook leaned toward the American Baptist Churches, while more conservative black Baptists felt more comfortable with the Southern Baptist Convention. In most cases racism prohibited a mass influx of black Baptists into the Southern Baptist Convention.

James Washington writes accurately of the "frustrated fellowship" of black Baptists.[14] There is an internal frustration, mainly due to political conflicts among powerful leaders. There is also an external conflict due to the racism so pronounced in white bodies. Theological understanding has little to do with such frustration. It is odd that the so-called Progressive Baptists have elected to secure the services of a very conservative press to produce their church literature. This assures that, except for top leadership, few authors of note will have any releases from that press. Black Baptist religious scholars must look elsewhere. This means that churchgoers will not be privileged to read some of the most gifted and profound writers among clergy and laity.

It is not necessary to critique black Methodists, since James H. Cone has done such a perceptive job in *For My People*.[15] My own encounter with leadership in black Methodist denominations has not been entirely edifying. Among clergy and laity, I have been greatly impressed by significant preaching, pastoring, and teaching. However, some of the leadership is so obsessed with the power of the episcopal office as to lose their sense of humanity and perhaps their faith also. The permission for the development of such a posture is given them by the people through the institutional structure. There have been strong racial leaders among these bishops for more than two hundred years. We are grateful for their bold and effective leadership. How much more could have been done on behalf of blacks if all the talented and gifted persons in the pulpits and pew had been set free with the support of these powerful leaders? If their commitment had been to servanthood rather than denomination, all their members would have been empowered in the quest of black freedom. Black bishops are not alone in their obsession for personal power. Baptist leaders are also known for this. We all need more humility and a sense of servanthood.

Black Theology and Ministry to the Underclass

Much of the black minister's time and effort go to the underclass. The underclass in the inner cities is almost another society, even beneath the working poor. It is an alternate society for those who have been shut out of the regular society. The tragedy is that it is growing perhaps faster than other parts of black society. While the number of whites in this category may be greater, the percentage of blacks sinking to this level of existence is reaching alarming proportions.

The social scientist William Julius Wilson has provided a definitive study on the underclass.[16] In his earlier *The Declining Significance of Race*, Wilson argued that the black community was becoming polarized, with an upwardly mobile black middle class that was sociologically distinct from a downwardly mobile black underclass.[17] While his black scholar peers found his discussion disturbing, it is obvious he put his finger on a reality that must be addressed.

Wilson focused on the social importance of economic forces. This economic factor in social life has often been overlooked by black theologians

The Prophethood of Black Believers

as well as black sociologists. Wilson's insights provided an important warning that economics play a powerful role in shaping human conditions. Wilson was also aware of a trend that many were unable to grasp—the significant effect of macroeconomics or economic structures on the plight of the black poor. However, since his book's title seemed to put economics above race as an explanation for black oppression, some did not read him as carefully as they should have.

Thus in his later work, his contribution is cast in clearer perspective. He wants to know why, in the face of antidiscrimination laws and their application, the plight of the black poor grows worse. He continues to lift up the benefits that are inherent to being of the black middle class. Affirmative action has aided those who were already prepared to take advantage of increased opportunities. The black poor have been bypassed. Wilson also makes a distinction between historic oppression of blacks and contemporary discrimination. He rightly insists that the history of oppression cannot be ignored if relief is to be significant in the present.

Wilson, in his later study, has helped us to understand the emergence of the black underclass. He also provides a powerful critique of the deficiencies in the liberal understanding of the underclass. The conservative religious and political forces have been able to misinterpret and exploit the situation in view of this liberal misunderstanding. Thus, he attempts to identify the obstacles to a persuasive liberal perspective, to address the problem of the ghetto underclass in a thorough analysis, and then to draw out the policy implications of his more comprehensive view.

According to Wilson, there are at least four important reasons why liberals fail to be as effective as they might be in addressing the underclass condition. First, they are careful in their interpretation for fear of blaming the victim and being charged with racism. Hence, they are reluctant to speak frankly. This reticence creates an opportunity for conservatives to step in and provide their own interpretation as well as influence policy decisions adverse to the needs of the underclass. Second, liberals refuse to use the word *underclass*. If the term is used at all, it is applied exclusively to individual characteristics, while it needs to be related to broader problems of society. These two limitations of the liberal perspective are foundational, but they point to other defects in the liberal view.

The third reason is that liberals accept selective evidence that denies the existence of an urban underclass. This shortcoming may even stem from an overemphasis upon the positive aspects of black experience. The pathological aspects may be seen as functional or adaptive patterns. In this effort to glorify blackness, the attention of policymakers may be diverted from the economic aspects of the problem. Black theologians and social scientists are often involved in this aspect of liberalism, as defined by Wilson. The fourth and final deficiency in the liberal perspective is that racism is used to explain all inner-city dislocations. Wilson seeks a relation between racism and poverty among blacks, but he insists that the emergence of the black underclass cannot be reduced to race alone. The status of the black underclass is related to the complexity of the present economic problems. The situation goes beyond the liberal explanations of the economic structure of racism. The problem lies with national and international economic organization, as well. Race remains a significant part of the problem, but the approach to the problem is multidimensional.[18] Wilson writes:

> Thus, rather than talking vaguely about an economic structure of racism, it would be less ambiguous and more effective to state simply that a racial division of labor has been created due to decades, even centuries of discrimination and prejudice; and that because those in the low wage sector of the economy are more adversely affected by impersonal economic shifts in advanced industrial society, the racial division of labor is reinforced.[19]

It takes courage for Wilson to treat the "social pathologies" among the underclass. He identifies some of these as follows: female-headed households, out-of-wedlock pregnancy, welfare dependency, unemployment, and interracial violent crimes.[20] Added to all of these pathologies is the use and selling of drugs. In the wake of this drug infestation, one sees the virtual destruction of an entire generation of young black people. There can be no real hope for a better condition for blacks, as a people, until these "pathologies" are frankly and forthrightly addressed.

Wilson has set us on a good path if we read his work carefully but also critically. Black ministers should read it in light of their experiences with the black middle class, the working poor, and the underclass. There are some intangible realities absent in Wilson's view of things that can be provided through the church's "resources of grace." Certain educative and value-clarification aspects of human life need to be brought in for consideration. The mission and ministry of black churches provide a powerful means to enrich, empower, and provide hope for the black poor and all conditions of black folk. A vital ministry to black people offers both the comfort and the strength needed to not merely survive but prevail.

Internal Prophecy

Much of black theology and preaching has been prophetic. This has been true throughout African American history. Contemporary black pastors have received great inspiration through the witness of Dr. Martin

Luther King Jr., among others. But we have majored in what I will call "external prophecy." We have directed the message of social justice to the white oppressor. Many tomes by black theologians register this message of protest against white racists. Since racism is still alive and well, this clarion call for justice must be sounded forth louder and clearer than before. We must not backtrack in racial progress. The black church and pulpit must always be outspoken in word and deed wherever there are injustices. This is our heritage and our destiny.

At the same time, we must look internally. We have become a self-destructive people. The plight of black males in the prime of life is very disturbing. A high percentage of our young men are incarcerated in the prison system. Those who are not in prison account for a very high incidence of crime. Black males are bent on self-annihilation by means of homicide. Suicide is no longer an isolated event. Too many are involved in drug use and drug dealing. We need to understand both what is being done to blacks as well as what blacks are doing to themselves.

The drug dealing of black males is matched, increasingly, by the drug use of black women. The high frequency of teenage pregnancies assures a bumper crop of fatherless children who will be reared in impoverished female-headed households. This saturation of the ghetto by drugs has led to an epidemic of AIDS and "crack" babies.

The sins of the fathers and mothers are being visited upon the next generation. We face an intergenerational crisis of great proportions. Careful analysis and causal examination of our communities are called for. The black family as well as the community needs to be looked at within as well as without. A thorough diagnosis must precede any attempted remedy of the black condition.

It is time for *all* black people to become concerned and get involved. We must seek to preserve our communal life. Rugged individualism is not a luxury we can afford. Thus, the "haves" must reach out to the "have-nots." The "me" generation outlook has influenced too many black middle-class people. We need to close the ranks and see what we can do to lift the underclass from self-destruction and total ruin. We must not have our success at their expense.

With this challenge before us we must seek the ministry of the whole people of God, laity as well as clergy. Black churches cannot afford to be "class" churches. The spirit of the early church of Acts should be manifest in our midst. Black churches need to be sharing, caring fellowships. We need to adopt a sense of oneness in the family of God.

We must develop a prophetic message appropriate for our constituency. The prophetic word must also be directed to the black middle class. The knowledge and skills of this group must be directed toward uplifting the black masses. The black masses must not be "objects of mission"; they are to be brought into the fellowship and ingrafted into the life of the one household of faith. Thus, the minister may be just as prophetic when he or she challenges the black middle class to witness in word and deed in the black community as when he or she addresses the injustices of the white community. The minister is to address injustice and indifference wherever it exists. There is a need for a powerful witness of the black churches in solidarity with the black masses.

Summary

The ministry in the black church is a peculiar ministry, unique and of special challenge. For this ministry, Black Theology is very important in both the academy and church. It is sometimes more important for whites than it is for blacks. It helps all Christians understand the Christian faith and the effective witness of churches in the United States. Black theologians and pastors should reflect and work together for a more effective witness in the black church. In this chapter, I have stressed the social teachings of black churches and noted the strong concerns for social issues in our mission due to the oppressed conditions based on slavery and racial discrimination. I have related black theology to the status of the black masses. Finally, I have described the prophetic work of ministry to internal as well as external situations of injustice and indifference. The nature and purpose of ministry is to be viewed against this background.

3

The Prophethood of Black Believers

BLACK THEOLOGY HAS ALWAYS BEEN A THEOLOGY of protest against social injustices. This protest or "radical" aspect of black theology has not always been conscious and widespread. Gayraud Wilmore, the historian of the recent Black Theology movement, made this radical element in the black church tradition explicit. His work has been followed by that of a number of black theologians who have engaged in black theological construction, following the leadership of James H. Cone. Joseph Washington had earlier identified black religion as a unique experience of religion by African Americans as compared with white Protestants and Jews.[1]

It is a misnomer to describe black religion, the black church, and black theology only in terms of emotionalism and healing. The black church was born in protest against racism. It first had to confront the brutal system of chattel slavery. Since discrimination based on race has continued, the protest character of black religion/theology persists.

In the experience of an oppressed group all concerns involve more than the well-being of the individual. Personal problems often stem from evils in the macrosystems of societal oppression. This is true of all races and classes in the United States. Thus, as I wrote in 1974, the matter eventually has to be addressed in structural terms:

> A black political theology provides a theological foundation for an action-oriented people who are determined to be black and free. This theology emerges out of the dark night of the black soul's distress. We seek the deliverance of a people as well as personal liberation. We will have the dignity of sons [and daughters] of God here and now. Therefore, black political theology has more to say about the salvation of blacks-in-community in this life.[2]

25

The Situation 1955–1975

The civil rights movement was a watershed effort to win the civil rights of African Americans. The movement was forged mainly in terms of political and legal rights. It was launched by the Supreme Court school desegregation decision of 1954. This effort was reinforced by congressional legislation as well as presidential directives. All branches of the national government joined in the support of civil rights for all citizens of the United States. When necessary, the military was used to enforce law and order. America appeared to be serious about bringing freedom to all Americans as a result of these decisions and actions.

In this climate, Martin Luther King Jr. began his work. It seemed to be a providential moment in history for his ethical and theological witness. He saw it as the right time to act. King called this period the *zeitgeist* or the spirit-of-the-time, a time for freedom. He associated it with what was happening in the entire third world as one European power after another gave up its colonies. It was indeed a time of *kairos*, a time of challenge, decision, and opportunity to bring freedom with the backing of the black church. Though King earned his graduate degrees at white liberal institutions, he had his anchor in the black family, church, and community. King was an able theologian and a powerful orator. Thus, he joined the legal and political flank of the civil rights movement. King was an avid supporter of the National Association for the Advancement of Colored People. He drew upon the spiritual and ethical dimensions of the black church tradition to provide a powerful battering ram against the evils of racism.

All Americans of good will had reasons to believe that race relations were changing for the better. Liberal Jews were very much a part of this effort to win freedom for blacks. Many white young people made the supreme sacrifice in this cause. However, by the middle '60s, things began to change for the worse. With the tragic deaths of Malcolm X and Martin Luther King Jr., the clouds of pessimism began to settle in upon the civil rights movement. Malcolm had advocated black nationalism and King the theory and practice of love as nonviolent action. With their deaths the black masses lapsed into a state of depression and hopelessness. Riots in more than one hundred cities dramatized this widespread despair.

A different outlook was emerging. It was the movement of black consciousness and black power. As early as 1966, black church leaders were developing an ecumenical consensus around "black power." Black young people in Student Nonviolent Coordinating Committee (SNCC) were embracing this new consciousness and power perspective. This new political and economic outlook was deeply rooted in black culture, which had

The Prophethood of Black Believers

been nurtured and sustained by black churches. While the church leadership was generally critical of the "violent" tone of the alternative movement, they saw in it constructive possibilities. Alex Haley's *Roots* conveyed the popular meaning of this search for peoplehood among blacks. Thus, a new consciousness and spirit was abroad in black communities. It cut out a new path of hope through the clouds of despair that had developed among the black people of this country.

Many important developments resulted from this new outlook. Black pride, a sense of identity and worth, was an important outlook. Out of a respect for the Afro-American past with its African roots came a powerful sense of peoplehood. The black church and black family, the music and other characteristics and gifts of blackness were now very precious. There developed many programs of self-help and self-determination in black communities. Black ministers and churches became more active in their leadership role to uplift black people. Black ecumenism transcended denominational affiliation as churches attempted to meet the this-worldly needs of their congregations. The purpose and mission of a black theology should be viewed in this context.

The Situation 1975–1991

During this critical period forces moved in two directions. On the one hand, the recent black consciousness/power outlook has been deepening its hold on upwardly mobile young people. The progress of the middle class has been aided by this new sense of pride of peoplehood. Through education, middle-class young people have been able to take full advantage of new opportunities where their knowledge and skills can be used. Affirmative action, providing new educational and job opportunities, has been extremely useful in stimulating and accelerating the upward mobility of blacks most disadvantaged.

Unfortunately, there has also been a movement in a reverse direction. It is a sad fact that white churches and white institutions have not maintained the moral high ground. The churches have followed the direction of secular leaders in the area of race relations. Reparations, payment of some compensation for past injustices, were considered for a brief period. Black theologians believed there were some biblical warrants for some compensatory action to correct the injustices with such a long history. This effort was stillborn. Early in the '70s there was talk of discrimination in reverse, that affirmative action for blacks was not merely illegal, it was immoral. There has been to my knowledge no concerted effort on the part of white churches to refute such an argument. Under the Republican national administration there was an attempt to dismantle every aspect of affirmative action in the name of a "color-blind" society. The self-righteousness of this effort has been unchallenged by white church bodies. In fact, it now seems to be generally accepted as the right point of view. Black intellectuals such as Thomas Sowell[3] and Walter Williams have been co-opted to support this view. Radical voices have been unheard or ignored. The nomination of Clarence Thomas to the Supreme Court is indicative of the mood.

Those blacks who are not able to overcome intergenerational oppression are cast aside. To the dismay of all, blacks as well as whites, the underclass is growing at an alarming pace. The actions of a sizable population of people are outside of acceptable social behavior. Blacks make up a too-high percentage of the members of this underclass. In an economy that requires an increasing amount of knowledge and skill, the underclass is not only unemployed but unemployable. Their creed is survival by any means necessary. The underground drug culture is the most glaring example of this tragic development. For the black youth caught up in this illegal underworld, life is short and brutal. At the same time the real kingpins of the drug underworld are not these poor black males. These young men are the subcontractors, the assassins, and the pitiable pawns in the service of the mighty and powerful barons of the worldwide drug network. If some of these young black males in the drug trade had an opportunity to get a college education, they could be respectable business leaders in this society.

To reclaim these lost youngsters and to keep others out of the illegal underground economy, we need to begin serious work with the very young. They will need education in more than math and science. They will need value clarification as well. Some will need to learn what it means to be a human being. They will need role models, and they will need to know that there is opportunity for a different life-style. The role of the black church is apparent. While the black church cannot assume this challenge alone, it has to be the motivator; otherwise we are in danger of losing several generations of young people.

The Black Church's Mission

We began this study with a theological discussion. As a minister and theologian I firmly believe in the divine appointment of the church. The church is God's "colony in the world." It has salvation of persons alienated from God's redemptive plan for human life as its first order of business. The church has a spiritual purpose and destiny. If we do not understand the nature of the church we cannot fully participate in its mission.

During a recent conversation with a Jewish layman and a rabbi, it occurred to me why black Christians love the Old Testament and have no real problem with the Jewishness of Jesus. The peoplehood of Israel, the providential guidance of God in the Old Testament, Moses the apostle of freedom, the prophets of social justice, the comfort of the psalms, the wisdom and suffering of Job culminate in the life and ministry of Jesus. The church is seen as the community that extends in this world the ministry of Jesus to the least and the lost. For black Christians the Jesus of history is the Christ of faith. As Dietrich Bonhoeffer has helped us to see, the Christ at the center of our faith is the earthly, concrete, empirical person in the midst of life, here and now. Thus, a vital conversation is possible with Jewish leaders who have a deep appreciation for Jesus as part of their heritage.

In this context, what leaped out at me was the similarity between the synagogue and the black church. Jews bring their sense of peoplehood into the community of faith. Not only is the biblical appeal similar for blacks and Jews, but also religion undergirds their sense of community.

The synagogue as an institution arose in the time of Babylonian captivity. The Hebrew designation *Beth Hakeneseth*, or House of Assembly, indicates its initial purpose. The synagogue was a rallying and worship center for an exiled people. The scriptures were read and expounded. Prayers were uttered and all aspects of worship developed. Instruction in Hebrew scripture took place.[4] Jewish law covers all aspects of personal and community life. The synagogue was a centering place for homeless people. In the absence of the temple, where the focus was upon outward forms of sacrifice and the written law, the synagogue became a place where the "inner Torah" nurtured a suffering people. In the time of the Diaspora, the Jews, an oppressed people, found the synagogue to be a center for all important activities. The rabbi, in time, carried forth from this center a whole ministry for a suffering people. The God who was interpreted there was one who cares and provides for the people. This faith is also an atoning and eschatological faith. The mission of the family and synagogue were mutually enriching.

In a similar way, we may describe the nature and mission of the black churches in African American history. We have already said something about the black church tradition. Through comparing it with the nature and mission of the synagogue, as briefly described here, we may gain a deeper appreciation of the biblical grounds for the black church and its mission. The black church, like the synagogue, is the center of life for many black people. It nurtures and sustains them psychologically and spiritually. In some cases there is provision for food, shelter, and health. All the concerns for the nurture of the young—their education, talent, and skill development—are high priorities. The empowerment of families is of great moment to a vital ministry in a black congregation. We might gain much by numbering our members by families, as some rabbis do, rather than by individuals. Black evangelism could be a powerful force if we sought to bring families into the larger family, the church. In this way black churches could greatly increase their effectiveness in the transformation of the total society.

The Nature of Ministry to the Dispossessed[5]

First we must determine what the self-definition of the oppressed community is. Who are we as black Americans? The titles we accept reflect a deeper identity crisis.

During my lifetime we have been called colored, Afro-American, Negro, black, and African American. It is necessary to sort all this out. In the self-appellation is hidden an ideology that determines our total worldview.

During the Negro period, I was not in any sense actively an exponent of radical social change. Ministry tied me to the concerns of the black masses. Personally, I was an intellectual bent on integration into the American mainstream.

The black power/black consciousness movement "aroused me from my dogmatic slumber." I experienced an intellectual and psychological conversion. This was to be translated into my role as a minister-theologian. The radical nature of the change that came over me led me to think profoundly about life experience and this altered my total worldview.

A serious engagement with the significance of my self-definition was necessary to withstand the rejection and misunderstanding resulting from this new perspective. It was important to work through the implications of black consciousness and power in order to interpret them. But it was of foremost importance to be able to live and act out of a new perspective of the self and society as an African American. In time, blackness carried for me a profound meaning as I knew my personal existence and as I reflected upon the peoplehood of black people in a racist society. Blackness implied several important things. It meant that I had a noble African ancestry. I celebrated the Afro-American past (with focus on achievement and protest against injustices). There was the extended-family tradition, which I came to appreciate. And there was the profound religious and church tradition that I was to interpret as a theologian. Accepting *blackness* was not easy, but once its meaning unfolded, it had a profound impact on my life-style and total outlook.

Having described the meaning for me of blackness, albeit briefly, I find recent African American self-designation somewhat troublesome. I am trying to come to terms with it, since the media and the publishing industry seem to consider the change a *fait accompli*. The only way I am able to use it meaningfully is to *think* through it critically.

The first time the term "African American" came to my attention was through statements made by Jesse Jackson. After visiting Africa, he desired to make the point that while in the United States blacks are in a minority, in Africa they are a majority. If we add the "colored" people in the entire Southern Hemisphere to the population in Africa, whites are indeed a small minority on this planet. This statement by Jackson, like so many others, had a political motivation. Therefore, I was not convinced.

My suspicions were upgraded by a poll reported by a Washington, D.C., newspaper during 1993. It indicated that most blacks still want to be called "black." It also stated that certain politicians like Jackson and William Gray preferred "African American." Since these persons are politicians as well as ministers, I still needed to continue my reflection. I wanted to know what is the meaning and value of this change from black to African American. What does it mean or matter to the average black person, especially the underclass without a sense of future? Blackness had begun to mean something to the black masses. It indicates self-pride and self-determination, among other things. Jesse often says, "Keep hope alive!" Does the use of "African American" assist in this endeavor?

Black scholars who are Afrocentric in outlook may contribute to this discussion. Persons like Molefi Kete Asante of Temple University as well as Asa Hilliard of Georgia State University may certainly use this self-designation with profound meaning. Arguing, for example, that human civilization started in Africa can give those informed by these African American studies a psychological lift.

This Afrocentric ideology has had profound impact on some black intellectuals. It has begun to affect schoolchildren through education. Hilliard takes elementary and high school black teachers on regular seminar trips to Egypt and other African countries. Asante, as head of Temple University's African American Studies Department, is making a profound impact on young black scholars and on education as well. Thus, Asante and Hilliard, among others, are giving educational and cultural importance to what in Jesse Jackson's outlook was mainly a political idea.

Leon Sullivan, through Opportunities Industrialization Centers International, is conducting programs in the heart of Black Africa. These are mainly educational and agricultural projects. However, since he holds conferences and airlifts hundreds of blacks to Africa to see their motherland, his efforts have broad implications. His program touches mainly the black middle class who are able to pay for the trip. After being with

Sullivan in Togo, I can personally attest to his vision and the profound impact of his effort upon Africans and Afro-Americans. "Afrocentric" takes on a concrete expression under Sullivan's leadership.

To bring this discussion to a head, I will briefly describe where I am on this subject and why. As a minister-theologian who is concerned about dialogue (both interreligious and intercultural), I can begin to use "African American" in a useful way. In this time of pluralism (local and universal), this terminology may say something about blacks that needs to be said.

The United States is becoming more conscious about its multicultural population. A large percentage of our citizens will be nonwhite by the year 2000. Nonwhite minorities are going to be powerful politically if not economically. As they become empowered they will no longer be ignored. Hispanics are already flexing their political muscle. Asians are excelling academically and economically. Thus, Americans can no longer think only in terms of black and white. Blacks are now in a situation of pluralism that includes not just Europeans but nonwhite groups. This pluralistic situation is the context for our decision and action.

As a minority with a long history in this country, we have much to offer the nation and we have important hindsight to share with other oppressed groups for their liberation. Thus, the term "African American" can have meaning for us in two directions. It makes us aware of a peoplehood rooted in a long heritage going back to Africa, just as others look back to Europe or Asia. It also provides an equal status for blacks in the multicultural mosaic of American society, where we share with others the culture of this country. This location of blacks in the context of pluralism has political and economic significance. If this hyphenated self-definition can help unite black people and lead them to join with other oppressed groups for a common liberation, it will serve us well. It is in some sense a name given to us by the media. Only if we can internalize for ourselves a profound self-understanding will it be worth our acceptance.

In the meantime, I will continue to use both "black" and "African American." It does not seeem wise to exchange a term that has grown in meaning to such a deep level for one that is still struggling to be born in my consciousness.[6]

Civil Rights and Economic Factors as Examples

Each year the Urban League provides an account of the condition of black Americans. President John E. Jacob opened the 1991 report with the sober reminder that "racism continues to extract a high price for African Americans and from the nation as a whole." He continued:

The Prophethood of Black Believers

Unfortunately, an important opportunity to remove discrimination barriers to the maximizing of all our human resources was lost when the president vetoed the Civil Rights Acts of 1990 and the Senate failed by only one vote to override the veto.

The Civil Rights Act of 1990 was urgently needed to correct several U.S. Supreme Court decisions that drilled loopholes into existing antidiscrimination laws.[7]

If the legal and political systems provided a setback, the economic situation in 1991 was equally dismal. In this same Urban League report, Professor David H. Swinton, who teaches economics at Jackson State University, points to the intergenerational disadvantages that racism has meted out to blacks. The low levels of ownership and the lack of control of business and other economic institutions account for much of this economic disability. The laissez faire policies of a market economy have resulted in the perpetuation of a disadvantaged economic status for blacks.

Swinton's report is supported by quantifiable research on such matters as employment, ownership, family income, and wealth. The bottom line of his study is:

The disadvantaged economic status of the African American population is a permanent feature of the American economy. The permanence of this disadvantaged status implies that it is perpetuated by the normal operations of the American economy. Thus, in the absence of strong and consistent intervention, we can project continued poverty and inequality as the permanent economic status of the African American population.[8]

The "invisible hand" of capitalism has not been kindly disposed toward people of color in the United States. For about four centuries, beginning with forced slavery for a long period followed by consistent discrimination, the economy of this country has had an adverse effect upon African Americans. Thus, if there is to be radical change for the better, there must be conscious, consistent, and vigorous efforts by blacks and others to alter this tragic situation. We call for improvement in the economic status of blacks in the interest of uplift and not for greed.

The Urban League report concludes with some important recommendations. It makes the point that America cannot reach its goal as a world leader without upgrading its nonwhite population. America's hope lies in its ability to achieve racial parity and to make use of African Americans and other minorities it has so long rejected. There is also a call for the black middle class to unite with the black masses for the liberation of all blacks. All must seek fairness, justice, and equal rights for the oppressed.

America cannot prosper for long if it allows more and more blacks to sink into illiteracy, poverty, and dependence. It must invest in human resources, assure quality education and job training opportunities, and bring neglected minorities into the productive mainstream.[9]

Implications for Ministry

It is well known that the black religious protest tradition has been attracted to the Old Testament, particularly the exodus account and the words of the prophets of social justice. One need only listen to black sacred music. The prayers and sermons in the black church attest to the same protest tradition. Too often there is a misreading of black worship. Some observers conclude that the ultra-emotionalism in some black churches can mean only a sheer other-worldliness. In most black churches and among most black ministers, the concern for social justice as a religious and moral obligation lies latent beneath the surface. It does not take much injustice to raise the ire of black ministers and laypersons alike when their rights as human beings are being violated. Black churches often champion the cause of the black masses.

What I want to make clear is that the cry for justice is always present in black churches. There are biblical and theological grounds for this appropriate response to mistreatment and injustice. In many books and articles, I have written about the quest for dignity on the part of black people, so I offer here only a brief summation.

We discovered wholeness as well as liberation in our search for African roots of black religion. The extended family was also reclaimed for the home and the church. Very early the Old Testament appealed to black slaves. Black preachers sometimes learned to read by searching the scriptures. They had a different worldview from their oppressors and they honestly sought a word from God. Theirs was a liberating interpretation of the entire Bible.

The exodus and the leadership of Moses stirred their imaginations and gave them hope of deliverance. This freedom was to be assured by divine action. Blacks believed that God is a great liberator of enslaved people. The providential guidance and succor of God gave them strength for a cruel existence. The communal nature of their African roots gave the slaves a deep appreciation for God as Lord of history. They believed that God is sovereign in creation and history. God has the power to rule and overrule in human affairs. In spite of their undeserved suffering as a people, God cares and God will win out. The purposes of God will eventually triumph over the evil designs of sinful humans. The message of the spirituals provides a close-up look at the sustaining faith in God held by black slaves. They were able to hope when there was no empirical basis for hope. There was a theology of hope in the black religious tradition long before Jurgen Moltmann made this notion famous. Moltmann clarifies this faith as he indicates that such hope is grounded in the promises of God. In the final analysis black hope is based upon a profound understanding of the promises of God, so that the God of hope is really a promise-keeping God.

The priority for black religionists has been the prophetic and succoring message of the Book. Therefore, the battle of the Bible (over a literal understanding of scripture) has never and is not now a priority for black biblical scholars and theologians. The prophetic word of social justice and the healing, comforting word of the psalmist have a special place for the black believer's faith. People that suffer from racism, a systemic form of evil with institutional expression, need a message of deliverance. They need to hear that God is just and that God runs history. Because of the interrelationship of structural evil and personal suffering from injustices, there is also a great need to know that God is a shepherd who "carries the young ones in his bosom." Black sufferers need to know of the compassion and mercy of God. Both the prophetic and priestly aspects of the gospel are important.

As we turn to the New Testament, we observe the unique place of Jesus in the black church. Listening closely to some black gospel music, one might think the black church borders on a worship of Jesus, a Jesus-ology, apart from a faith in God. It is true that black gospel music writers need to sit down with black scholar-pastors as well as theologians. There is a need for serious theological reflection as we write black music for black churches. This is another subject that needs intense discussion, but in another context. Nevertheless, black music does lift up the attractiveness of Jesus in black churches.

Jesus is so affirmed because he is perceived as both prophet and priest in black belief. Both these roles are important for a people suffering from systemic evil as well as from evils of a personal nature. Both forms of the experience of evil must be addressed by our faith. The earthly Jesus is a human being of "flesh and bone." Jesus, according to black belief, is a divine friend near at hand. Through the ministry of Jesus on earth God is approachable. As Bonhoeffer said, God is "have-able." The incarnation is concrete and empirical in black faith. If there is a weakness in traditional black belief, it is the absence of a strong emphasis upon "the Christ of faith." There is a great need for forging a powerful christological statement that reconciles for black Christians the significance of both aspects of the Christian doctrine of Christ—that the Jesus of history is the Christ of faith. Only thus can the strong affection for Jesus be rooted in a total faith in the God of Jesus.

Again this discovery of Jesus as one who identifies with the weak and needy has a significance for a prophetic theology in the face of systemic injustices. There is a need for a "political" as well as a "salvific" reading of the cross and resurrection of Jesus. Thus, the tendency in Barth and Bultmann to play down the earthly Jesus must be rejected. The saving proclamation of the gospel includes the life and ministry of Jesus on earth prior to the climactic summing up of his redemptive mission in the cross-resurrection event. A real incarnation includes the total enfleshment of God in the earthly Jesus. His death "under Pontius Pilate" makes a political statement. His birth, his witness among the dispossessed, his preaching to the poor, his visits to prisoners, his healing ministry are all part of the gospel. To Jesus, sin and evil, the temptations "that all flesh is heir to," were real. He opposed evil in high places, in Jewish circles as well as in Roman circles. But it was the sins of the entire human family that led him to his death on a cross. Jesus confronts the powers of evil and death. But God raised him. This is the stuff out of which a secure faith is born. My reading of black faith leads me to believe that the substance of a profound faith is there in outline, but it needs a more coherent and consistent interpretation. To meet this need black theologians are called to their servanthood to Christ and the church.

There are many devout black Christians who earnestly seek to do the will of God yet who do not see that black religion has an inherent prophetic strain. A deacon, who is the chair of a board in a major congregation, recently told me that he did not want his pastor to get involved in community affairs outside the church. The pastor had taken up gay rights and desired to run for a seat on the city school board. It was this deacon's candid opinion that the pastor should direct all his attention to "churchly" affairs. It was clear to this deacon that if the pastor refused to be thus occupied, he should leave the pastorate for these other activities. Of course, there are outside limits to these types of community involvements. It is obvious that if outside involvements take priority or compromise the pastor's ethical position, then he or she should draw in and focus on the church's witness. But the concerns of this young seminary-trained minister seemed to be the usual ones for the black pastors for at least two hundred years. It occurred to me that this pastor needed to introduce his people, especially the leadership, to black church history and black theology. There is now much literature available and much of it is readable for laypersons in the black church. This teaching should in no way replace the strong emphasis upon the Bible study. It is, however, a necessary supplement.

A student of mine, a Lutheran pastor, completed his doctor of ministry thesis project on "the priesthood of believers." His study involved his lay leadership. The elders in his church evaluated a series of sermons he preached on this subject. He also held a series of class sessions on this subject. Before he submitted his thesis for final approval, he reported a phenomenal transformation in the understanding of his elders regarding their ministry in the church. If black pastors seek the prophetic role through which they endeavor to liberate their people, they will likewise need to find a way to teach their people some of the important aspects of black theology. The best way, it seems to me, would be to provide a study on the protest aspect of black religion, using music, prayers, sermons, and the like as resource materials. At the end the people should be introduced to the works of black theologians as well as some volumes by black pastor-scholars who have used black theology in various aspects of ministry. The pastor-scholars chosen as the Martin Luther King Jr. Fellows,[10] are excellent role models for such a project in the local church. I believe that the black deacon mentioned above would be "teachable" and that he and his pastor could work together if he were thus enlightened.

Another theological insight comes from other aspects of the New Testament, especially the writings of Paul. As a theologian, I do not believe that Paul's contribution to the understanding of the Christian faith should be ignored. I am aware that one of the greatest black religious scholars of this century, Howard Thurman, had a rather negative impression of Paul. His rejection of Paul was based upon his grandmother's recalling the "opiate" passages in Paul used by preachers representing the slave master's point of view. Many of us have had to refine our parents' and grandparents' faith through critical personal reflection. Thurman should have done just that. But Thurman did not consider himself a theologian. He was foremost a mystic and religious philosopher. It was not as difficult for him as it is for a black theologian of the church to dispense with Paul. I refuse to do so.

There is, however, a reading of Paul on the doctrine of justification that needs to be discussed. It is well known that because of Luther's reading of Paul, "justification by faith" became the rallying cry of the Protestant Reformation. Luther also wanted the book of James removed from the biblical canon because it speaks of "works" as well as "faith." We need to put Luther's position on justification in context. He was opposing one extreme with another. The Roman Catholic tradition of meritorious works and indulgences was being opposed by a total rejection of the human part in salvation. Thus, Luther's radical personal and theological position of justification by faith alone should be seen for what it is. We can also find in Paul grounds for sanctification in which human participation is involved.

In sanctification we find a foundation for growth in faith. Paul refers to development from infancy to adulthood in Christ. Christian living is fulfilled through a state of weakness to strength through grace. Grace is both prevenient and sanctifying in Paul's total outlook. There is a sense in which Christians "work out their salvation" at the same time "Christ works in and through us." We are laborers together with God. There is also a sense in which creation and redemption are brought together in Paul's understanding of God's salvific work in the world.

The whole creation is to be redeemed. Paul sees "principalities and powers" as agents of evil. Evil is structural, even cosmic. But Christ reigns "until all enemies" will be subject to his power. The resurrection symbolizes the defeat of sin and death, personal and social. Thus, a great deal of our understanding of faith as Christians comes out of a more critical and complete reading of Paul. In black faith, there is no sharp contradiction between the doctrines of justification and sanctification. Since the black pentecostal movement is growing faster than any other black church tradition, it is hoped that theologians in this tradition will take up the doctrine of sanctification and give it a more balanced interpretation in the future. In fact, the "progressive pentecostals" like James Forbes promise to do so.

Summary

In this chapter we have focused upon what was called "the prophethood of black believers." Throughout I have been concerned with the protest dimension of black religion, theology, and church. Without downgrading the healing, "priestly" aspects of black religion, I have rather been seeking a holistic balance. This chapter may be designated as a statement of "black political theology." Here I have sought to lift up the situation of unfairness that is the reality of black life. I am concerned about the black church's ministry of justice in an unjust society, filled with racism.

To provide a proper context for our discussion, I described the situation through historical references as well as the Urban League study of 1991, "State of Black America." This was followed by a focus on the mission of the black church as it confronts systemic evils. We saw some similarity between the Jewish and black religious tradition. We lifted up the role of the synagogue and the black church and also the ministry of black pastors and Jewish rabbis. Both have a high regard for the Hebrew Bible. A powerful ethical theology and sense of ministry is shared. Jesus figures largely in their mission and ministry.

Turning to the ministry to the dispossessed, we looked at the identity crisis of black people today. This was placed in historical perspective, but the emphasis was upon the present self-designation of black people.

Are they "black" or "African American"? In my judgment both terms are meaningful and have a place in our discussion. I pinpointed civil rights and economic deprivation as examples of racism and its oppression of blacks. There needs to be a concrete expression of how racism oppresses, and these examples are representative and important.

Finally, we turned to implications for ministry. I suggested that the black faith tradition has biblical and theological warrants for protest. I spent some time developing the scriptural and theological bases for a black theology. I concluded that this protest message against injustices is inherent in the history, theology, and mission of black churches, but it cannot be taken for granted. It is implicit, but not always explicit. For this reason black pastors have the responsibility to teach this prophetic message to their people. Sometimes lay people may impede the efforts of well-informed pastors because the laity may have a limited understanding of ministry and mission in black churches. At other times they may be moved against injustices but need more enlightenment regarding the biblical grounds for their work or the know-how of bringing about social liberation. In any event, the prophethood of all believers is so central to the black church's ministry that it should be forcefully sponsored for the sake of the liberation of black people in a situation of stifling racism. What this implies is that black churches must produce their own literature if they are to be set free from the one-dimensional gospel of many white churches in the same denomination. Indeed, it is unhistorical, unnatural, and self-defeating for black churches to be limited by the misinformation that curtails their liberation as sons and daughters of the Christ who sets us free.[11]

4

Education as Ministry

WITH SO MUCH EMPHASIS UPON PREACHING, BLACK ministers and their congregations often underestimate the role of education as a ministry. In this chapter I will seek to lift up the important place of education in the life of the church. Even so, this focus on education is taken within the wider frame of reference of the church.

Educational ministry provides an unusual opportunity for cooperative work between the pastor and others in the congregation. However, the leadership in this field, as in all other areas of ministry, will reflect the priorities set by the pastor in theory and practice. One of the critical marks of Protestantism is "the priesthood of all believers." Where a professional minister of education is not available, usually some person in the congregation can work with the pastor to provide an effective educational ministry. In black churches this concern should be lifted up often, in "pastoral observations" as well as in didactic sermons. The entire congregation should be moved by the pastor's passion for education in the fellowship.

What we have in mind here is more than traditional Bible study. Too often this consists of "sword drills," or committing favorite texts to memory. So far as Bible study is concerned, it is crucial that the classes be taught by well-informed teachers. If the pastor is the only seminary-educated person, he or she should teach the teachers. The pastor should be not only the motivator but also the enabler. A black pastor should carefully select the literature to be used. She or he should introduce materials by competent black scholars while screening all materials to be used.

Education, especially among the oppressed, should be more comprehensive than Bible study alone. It may include attacks on illiteracy for adults and tutoring of the young. Grammar and literacy skills should be stressed along with mathematics and science. Our church program of education should not neglect the humanities in favor of skills highly prized in a technological age. Education in our churches should provide an alternative to such lopsided education. The church should be a place where the ideas and values that provide meaning and direction to life should be encountered, if nowhere else. In most cases black people have lost the ability to direct the education of the young in public schools. The home and the church bear a heavy burden so far as the teaching of values is concerned.

The Pastor as Religious Educator

In our black church tradition we have majored in preaching. Often effective preaching has yielded a great success in member growth and the numbers who attend worship. Nevertheless, in many large black churches, the educational ministry is not present or is inadequate for the needs of the people.

Since pastoral leadership is key to all programs in black churches, the pastor must intervene in the educational ministry of the church if it is to be significant. He or she must insist that religious education is at the heart of the church's ministry. Our people are too often confused and unaware of the full gospel message for life and suffer from lack of teaching in our churches. Our sermons are often inspiring and uplifting, but without a vital teaching content.

Even when our sermons are didactic, there is no opportunity to appropriate the message through discussion. There is no "talk back" session and there is usually no opportunity to engage the preacher-pastor in a format where questions and answers are considered a normal exchange. The class setting provides opportunity for dialogue. People need to be able to bring their vital concerns from everyday life to the religious educator for reflection.

A few months ago, I was with a pastor of a major congregation who challenged his congregation to establish a broader educational ministry. He did not do this because his preaching is not effective. Neither was he concerned about a lack of attendance in Sunday school or Sunday worship. Many pastors would have been completely satisfied with things as they are in that church. But this pastor saw a deeper need. The congregation responded in full support of their pastor.

This pastor hired a full-time religious educator. He has a thriving Saturday School. On a recent assignment, I taught more than forty adults "Christian beliefs" on Saturday mornings over a period of several weeks. I was deeply moved by their thirst for knowledge and the lively exchange we had during the discussion periods.

Many educational programs are on the way at the Zion Baptist Church of Philadelphia, under the able leadership of Pastor Gus Roman. Roman is a model pastor-educator. He is not alone; several other pastors are taking the lead in educating their people. Yet there are not enough pastor-educators in black churches. What we need is a ground-swell movement nationwide to meet the needs of black people, especially the young.

The pastor-educator should always keep clearly before the congregation the idea that the goal of the Christian life includes concern for the liberation of an oppressed people. Grant S. Shockley has expanded this project of Christian education beyond the usual concerns. As a black educator in the church, Shockley has correctly indicated the need for religious education for social justice. All aspects of the Christian faith, including dedicated Christian living, must be part of the program. However, the issue Shockley addresses is critical for education and it is at once biblical and integral to the black church tradition. Shockley writes:

> Pastors have an exciting opportunity to model and stimulate others to become engaged in social justice ministries. . . . Such a social ministry must be undertaken in community with the laity who are involved in the very structures of society where they can make a difference."[1]

It follows that the role of the black pastor as educator goes well beyond the traditional role. It includes secular education, but majors in moral and spiritual values. Social justice is also of great concern.

Value Clarification and Religious Education

Before discussing further the significance of various approaches to religious education, we will introduce the meaning given to some key terms: *value*, *moral*, *education*, and *religion*.

Value comes from the Latin *valere*, "be worth." It is also close in meaning to "virtue," from the Latin *virtus*, which refers to worth or quality of life.

Moral refers to the right or the good in reference to standard of conduct or character. It comes from the Latin *mos* or *moris*, "manner." Moral can refer to customary rules and accepted standards of society. *Ethics*, closely related to moral, has to do with principles, or the study of principles, of right conduct. There is a branch of philosophy by that name.

Education comes from the Latin *educare*—*e*, "out," and *ducere*, "to lead"; hence, it means "to draw or bring out." Education is several things, traditionally: (1) process, (2) knowledge, (3) formal schooling, and (4) a systematic study of problems and theories of teaching, learning, or training. Education then, is the development of knowledge, skill,

The Prophethood of Black Believers

ability, or character through teaching, training, study, or experience. The term is also used to refer to the sciences and art that deal with the principles and problems of teaching, training, and learning.

Religion comes from the Latin *religio*, which means reverence for the gods, holiness in a system of religious beliefs (*re*, "back," and *ligare*, "to bind," hence, to bind together). Religion usually implies belief in a divine or superhuman power or powers to be obeyed or worshiped. It includes the expression of such a belief in conduct or ritual.

Having defined these key terms, let us now look briefly at some assumptions basic to our discussion.

First, humans have a great propensity for religious experience. Wholesome religious experience contributes to the enrichment, empowerment, and fulfillment of human life.

Second, people in our nation are presently faced with a crisis of value in their lives. Young people are confused about the distinction between value and disvalue. Many seem to be facing life situations with no obvious knowledge of the existence of value. This seems to be more pervasive among the very poor and the extremely rich. Yet a crisis of value is widespread in our midst and needs to be addressed.

Third, this discussion assumes that some moral standards need to be inherent in the educative process. Morals at their best are founded upon and sustained by religious roots. If these religious sources are diluted or neglected, morals will eventually dissipate—the substance of morality will be lost.

And fourth, human beings are born morally neutral. It is a categorical mistake to assert that humans are inherently good or evil. They are potentially either or both, depending upon nurture. It is precisely because of the potential of humans, as free but responsible selves, that moral education is so critical to their growth and development.

Many would agree that young people are growing up without role models and a system of values. Among young black males, there is a value crisis of gigantic dimensions. It is reflected in the craving for designer clothes, sports jackets, and sneakers. Many boys and young men of great potential have been killed over such items. Drug dealers have cashed in on the sneaker craze. Some maintain a closet full of sneakers to enhance their status.

Even role models like Spike Lee and Michael Jordan may be unwittingly reinforcing crass materialism. As millionaires, they are cashing in on a market that is destroying their own black brothers. A basketball player who achieves success does indeed inspire the ghetto youth to become a great athlete. However, since most will not make the grade in athletics, education leading to a degree is the better bet for most black males.

Companies are motivated only by the desire for profit. Operating within the American economic system, they use athletic stars and even Black English to promote their wares. Many young people from the ghetto are influenced to do whatever is necessary to obtain the advertised products as a statement or status symbol. This matter illustrates a major crisis. The problem is deeper than the desire for sneakers or other luxury items such as designer jackets and gold jewelry. We must recognize the real problem and introduce a program to teach and redirect the young to other goals that are more enduring.

Some urban pastors observe that underclass children they meet are without any knowledge of the Bible. They have never been to church. They are completely amoral, without a conscience or moral compass. Meaningful family life does not exist. Some are abandoned in the streets, never having been introduced to any religious source of ethics. Decisions are made according to the impulse of the moment. They are prepared to do whatever is necessary to survive in an urban jungle, without mercy or compassion. Even in our colleges we encounter young people who seem to be almost completely secular in orientation. They do not have the standards of any tradition of moral values as a basis for moral judgment and action.

In this context, we must look carefully at the drive for education in values or values in education. Some of the reasons given are noble—others are suspect.

There is grave concern in our nation about education, especially in regard to the quality of U.S. education as compared to that of other advanced societies. For example, some critics have mainly economic interests. They wish to push literacy in math and science for fear that the Japanese will outdo us.

For others, there is a deeper concern regarding our national moral crisis. We are faced with insider trading, lying, unbridled greed, and other evils based upon rugged individualism. Much of this can be traced to capitalism run amok. This situation has entrapped our brightest, finest, and best young people, including Harvard business school graduates.

Among all segments of our society we face a value crisis. If we look among the down-and-out or the underclass, too many of whom are black, we find widespread participation in the drug trade, prostitution, and other underground business enterprises. These illegal enterprises rival Wall Street in income yield. We speak of the underground economic activities of youth who are trapped in poverty, illiteracy, and lovelessness of our super-segregated ghettos.

In these urban crises, black and especially Hispanic youth are trapped in a situation without hope and no sense of future. Violence in the form of suicide, homicide, rape, and robbery are daily involvements. Crack babies, teenage pregnancies, infant deaths, child neglect and abuse, and similar tragedies are rampant. AIDS is an increasing scourge among heterosexuals as well as homosexuals in these situations. Many able, dedicated, and seasoned educators feel hopeless in their vocation. It is a major challenge to get a handle on how to educate children thus victimized by these plagues.

These issues reinforce the conviction that sinfulness is a reality in human nature. Furthermore, moral values have their grounding and sustenance in religious faith. No root, no fruit. Moral values may linger for a while after religious conviction wanes, but they will eventually fade away. And yet, I hold the conviction that human nature is "a good thing spoiled." In spite of sin, there remains a potential for good as well as evil.

Therefore, our discussion of the educative process will necessarily take into account religious experience. While the writings of thinkers like William James, John Dewey, and Emile Durkheim are instructive, they are not adequate for our purpose here. This is especially true of Dewey and Durkheim, who do not have a significant role for religion in their programs. James however, does deal with religious experience in a scholarly way. Our purpose is served best by Lawrence Kohlberg's moral development approach.

Let us look briefly at Kohlberg's contribution to our discussion.[2] His perspective on education is useful here because he lays the responsibility upon the school for the development of values. Because of the breakdown of the family, families have been unable to fulfill their roles in this regard. Another factor to be considered is that leadership in public schools has been taken from black principals and teachers, especially in the South. Those who pressed hardest for prayers in public schools may not see racial justice and social equality as a part of religion anyway, though they may be preoccupied with "family values" within the monocultural community to which they belong.

Kohlberg, like Dewey and Durkheim, insists upon the need for education as a transmitter of values in society. He views justice as the most fundamental of the values in a society.[3]

Kohlberg is seeking a universal basis for moral education similar to Kant's "categorical imperative." He does not mean "character education," which is intended to instill a specific moral principle, like honesty, in a child. The goal of moral education is to stimulate the natural development of the individual child's moral judgment. Kohlberg wants to arouse the child's own capacities of moral perception, leading to the proper maturation and to use of that inherent potential to control behavior. Again, moral education is the stimulation of development rather than the teaching of fixed virtues. The child is aided by the educative process to move to the next step of moral judgment in the direction toward which she or he is already tending. Nothing from outside is imposed on the child. The sense of justice is inherent in human nature as such.

Justice, according to Kohlberg, is respect for the rights of others, based upon consideration of equality and reciprocity. He sees the American value of liberty as included in his notion of justice. Justice also includes benevolence—the consideration of the welfare of all other individuals.

This conception of moral development coincides with a culturally universal definition of morality. It transcends adherence to the content of specific moral beliefs. Kohlberg indicates that this view has been empirically tested in Russia, Israel, Turkey, Italy, and Mexico, among other places. He insists, therefore, that his outlook is cross-cultural, inter-religious, as well as nonreligious. He concludes that the moral development of a child does not depend upon a particular religious belief system. He agrees that religions usually have an associated moral code, but moral judgment may influence religion as much as the other way around. Moral judgment, he argues, is independent of religion. The educative process does, however, play a positive role in stimulating moral development. Thus the curriculum requires explicit educational thought about the moral objectives of education.

Kohlberg identifies three levels with five stages of moral development. The levels and stages are as follows: Level I includes stage 1, punishment and obedience orientation, and stage 2, instrumental-relativist orientation. Level II includes stage 3, meeting external expectations, and stage 4, law and order. Level III has stage 5, self-chosen moral principles. Originally, Level III had two stages—social contract or utility principle, and universal ethical principle, which was exemplified by Gandhi, for example. In sum, Level I is preconventional, Level II is conventional, and Level III is postconventional.[4]

Some questions may be raised about Kohlberg's proposal:

1. How does action flow from moral knowledge? We cannot wait until a child reaches the "principles" stage (stage 5) to deal with behavior. There needs to be a correlation between knowledge and action at every stage.
2. Kohlberg claims that his stages are scientific as well as universal. This is well and good, but where does experience come in? Experience as well as knowledge can aid more perception. For example, an older child, with more experience, may arrive at a higher level of moral perception through that experience without depending upon cognitive development.
3. Who decided that *justice* is the virtue that is all-inclusive? We need a more convincing argument.

The Prophethood of Black Believers

4. His approach is extremely *cognitive* and *individualistic.* How can this method embrace the whole person and influence all behavior? While we see several influences that would balance his position, he seems too independent in his emphasis.

Kohlberg would argue his point in this way. Justice is understood from the vantage point of moral development. It is not a given value, which can be concretely transmitted to or imposed on children. It is, however, the basic valuing process that underlies each person's capacity for moral judgment. Justice is that native sense of *fairness,* which gives form to how individuals make judgments of right and wrong. To "teach justice," then, involves helping students develop an increasingly more adequate sense of fairness.

He provides, as he sees his role, a way to teach moral values without imposing them on children. By promoting their native sense of fairness, the teacher is not imposing any value content on the students. The teacher is, rather, preparing them to comprehend and appropriate more fully the principle on which the moral philosophy of the Constitution of the United States is based. Kohlberg lifts up the Constitution as a kind of transcendent norm for ethical values in American society.

As we have observed, justice is a universal moral principle that any morally mature person in any society should use as a basis for making moral judgments. Thus the aim of this moral development approach is not limited to the goals of American education. It extends to include the goals of global citizenship.

In order to establish his claim more securely, Kohlberg compares his developmental approach with three other alternative theories or procedures: the *romantic,* the *cultural transmission,* and the *progressive* approaches.

1. The romantic approach seeks to develop in students values and skills that will contribute to achieving a psychologically healthy and self-fulfilling life-style.
2. The cultural transmission outlook seeks to teach students behaviors and attitudes that reflect the traditional values of their society.
3. The progressive perspective is designed to teach students skills in order to live more effectively and successfully as members of their society.

The moral development plan, on the other hand, is intended to promote the development of the student's *capacities* in areas of cognitive, social, moral, and emotional functioning.

Thus, the choice of the developmental approach to moral growth is based upon two assumptions: first, that it has intrinsic worth, and second, that it is usually irreversible in time. Teaching students to clarify values and to develop to a higher stage of moral judgment is a process that contains its own moral ends. If one can buy into Kohlberg's assumptions regarding justice, his thesis, and the inherent potential for goodness in human nature, then his proposal is a compelling one. His position is weakened if one cannot agree with any or all of his assumptions.

As a minister-theologian, I would insist that religions in relation to moral development are important for several reasons. First, most religions are foundational to and sustain a significant moral core of meaning. Once you dismiss these religious foundations, you weaken the moral core. Over time, the moral core could also disappear. For instance, many religions nurture and sustain "a principle of humanity" that upholds the dignity and worth of human life. Something like the Golden Rule is present. The Decalogue as well as Christian ethics in the natural law tradition are morally compatible with the United Nations Declaration of Human Rights.

Second, religions have a deep insight into human nature that is indispensable to moral development. It seems to me that it is a mistake to entrust the meaning of human nature to scientists, even social scientists. Even Marxists (revisionists) are beginning to realize that there is a "transcendent" dimension to human life that is absent from what they have referred to as "a species-being." Human life seems to have existential, cultural, and other aspects that their economic-materialistic conception of human life has missed. What religions say about humans who are to receive moral education is vital and invaluable.

Third, religion brings a different understanding about the temporal perspective. Whereas scientists look to the future, religion and ethics depend greatly upon hindsight as a basis for foresight. As we seek religious and ethical insight for the young, it is essential to mine the deep deposit of moral resources, much of which goes back to historical periods before the time of Jesus in many cultures and not just our own. This is true whether we are Jewish, Buddhist, or Confucian—certainly moral teachings of a Judeo-Christian-Greco-Roman outlook must take seriously the religious and ethical foundations rooted in the past. There is a *timelessness* as well as a *universality* involved.

Finally, there are many hurdles to overcome if we are to teach religion or moral values associated with religion in public schools. Much discussion is misplaced. The issues are usually church-state, constitutional issues (focus on Bible reading and prayer, for example). The more fundamental issue of moral development is often missing. Kohlberg attempts to make a case for moral instruction in public schools by arguing that the Constitution itself is not morally neutral. Insofar as he separates morality from religion, he does not help on the religious front. For some, "released time" for religious instruction seems to be legally acceptable. However, legal action by atheistic or agnostic parents or the American Civil Liberties Union could challenge this in court. In view of the position that religions are important to moral development in the young as well as the old, I would propose that public schools teach *about* religion. It is possible to include religious and moral insights in the study of subjects such as literature, art, and music. In fact, religious and moral values are abundant in a study of the humanities and the fine arts in general. A comprehensive study of our heritage is not possible without such exposure. The preparation of future teachers to pursue this task should not be left to colleges and universities alone. Here is a unique opportunity for seminaries to serve the academy as well as the churches in the transmission of religious as well as ethical values.

The Educational and Teaching Ministry of Black Churches

Teaching or education must become central to the black church's mission. Education must not be neglected even in the name of political activism. There is no substitute for intellectual enlightenment for those who would be free.

A people who would become subjects rather than objects of history must strive to become well informed through education. Oppressors know this. This is why slave masters sought to deny black slaves the opportunity to learn to read and write. Without knowledge the mind is enslaved and the oppressor can remove the eternal chains. Knowledge and freedom are noble companions.

The mass media give most attention to the worst that happens in the black community. In general the media seem almost to celebrate the worst expressions of sex and violence in the society at large. Seldom is anything positive or uplifting reported from the black community.

In a newspaper release, theologian Avery Dulles made an important observation.[5] In our feverish attempt to eliminate religion from all public instruction, he said, we are establishing secularism by default. Whether we like it or not, political judgments are permeated with moral and religious assumptions. He asserts that the church makes its best contribution to society by nurturing personal faith and morality.

Behind this assumption by Dulles is the belief that humans can be nurtured in moral and spiritual matters. Another way of stating the case is to assert that human beings can be instructed. Such instruction is by educative procedures and by example. Lest we lapse into hopelessness, given our serious human condition, we must be assured of the constructive process. As we turn to education as a means to social liberation from our many ills, we need to keep certain concerns before us.

First, we assume that education, in a comprehensive sense, can make a difference in our crisis situation. Whether the crisis is AIDS or wanton violence, we look to education as a way out. Education is viewed by many as the foundation for any semblance of civilized life in community. As a strong believer in education, I would offer a word of caution. Education should not be viewed as a panacea. The type of education and the deliverer determine to a great extent its constructive effects. Education is an important means for intervention provided it is carried out in the proper manner.

Second, education needs to include moral values, since so many of our problems have moral implications. For instance, as important as the computer is as a means to share information, it can never be an end. The introduction of "computer viruses" by some of our brightest youth is a symptom of a moral disability wherever we rely on technical know-how. We as a nation are the victims of internal moral decay, which must be urgently and decisively addressed through moral education and other means as well.

Third, education is a form of *nurture*. This concept needs to be developed a little further for emphasis. There are those who place most of their stress on *nature* or genetics as determinative of the development of human beings. In my judgment, there is sufficient ground to insist that maturation—intellectual, moral, psychological, and physical—is influenced by social and environmental factors. Human potential can *grow* or *develop* if there is a proper nurturing process at work. Human beings are teachable through word and deed. How we rear and educate the young makes a difference in determining who humans will become. What we know about human life through educational and social science research supports this view. We, therefore, assume "that as a twig is bent, the tree is inclined."

Yet education itself can become mis-education. This is true of religious education as well as secular education. We need to guard well what we use as literature in black churches. We need to raise up a generation of religious educators who will do the research and writing of our own church literature.

A great deal of progress among blacks in a few generations has been due to a thirst for knowledge. I recently read a collection of slave narratives. The autobiographical accounts had one thing in common. They all indicate that slaves were forbidden to read and write. This very prohibition may have fueled the determination of the freed men and women to seek education. Even parents who were illiterate or who had limited schooling sought to send their children to college. They often implanted in their youngsters a determination to be educated.

The Prophethood of Black Believers

In some extended families, this drive for education became contagious. Brothers, sisters, and even cousins gave one another a helping hand as entire families sent all youngsters off to college. The extended family served us well as we strove to educate our young. We believed that education was one of the great liberators of our people. Education, we believed, was one important road to freedom. But we were aware that it was not a panacea. Churches and religious institutions were and still are the sponsors of educational pursuits.

We seem to have lost much of this thirst for knowledge. Family life is no longer the force that it was. We can no longer assume that a family is behind a young person seeking education. We have become selfish and greedy like many in our social environment. What we learn on the streets and over television reinforces these negative trends. Young blacks grow up without a developed conscience and without value clarification. Until now, our churches have not helped much. Religious education has not been our strong suit. Bible study needs to be undergirded by strong ethical teaching and personal example.

Desegregation of schools has met with white resistance since 1954. The power arrangements have been altered but decisions are now even more in white hands. The children have been mixed, but because of segregated housing, macroeconomics, and administrative setups, blacks now have even less input into the educational process than in pre-integration days. Our young no longer have black teachers and counselors who are also the pillars of our churches. The secular views in our schools are central. In some cases white teachers and principals discourage our children. White teachers sometimes have a low estimation of the potential of black youth and direct them into vocations where they can use their hands rather than their brains.

On this I can speak with some authority from concrete personal observation. As a native North Carolinian, I am in and out of the state several times a year. On one occasion, a retired black principal, later a county commissioner, observed that blacks now have only their churches and families as institutions to prepare their young. He had been one of the few black principals to retain his position after the desegregation of the schools in that state. He was thus in a position to see firsthand how black students and teachers were mistreated in the desegregation process. Several newspaper editorials in North Carolina have lamented the shortage of black teachers. The state board of education indicates that something must be done to increase the number of black teachers. Absent is the account of why there is this lack. No mention is made of the systematic program to dismiss and demoralize a whole generation of black educators. For example, when black teachers retire they are consistently replaced by white teachers. These and other actions drove a host of black teachers, counselors, and principals out of education. It also discouraged black college students from studying education. All these things have had a disastrous effect upon the impressionable minds of black young people.

This process has continued for several decades now with devastating effect. Formerly black schools had played a positive role in discovering and developing talented black girls and boys for effective leadership and responsible citizenship. Those with bright minds and good character were encouraged to continue to study and develop themselves for future responsibilities. However, in this new climate many were advised not to go to college. If they were to continue their studies, they should go to a trade school. Role models became scarce and counselors negative, if not hostile. Only strong individuals were able to excel and sustain their determination. Black students with real abilities were passed over for honors and key leadership roles. The support system they needed was wiped out. The dropout rate and the total failure of many could have been foreseen by whites, who set in motion this devious scheme. It was carefully designed and systematically carried out. The present lack of black teachers is the inevitable result. It was the conscious, malicious misdirection of the desegregation program by those in power that led to these consequences. These results have an adverse impact on all the people of North Carolina. This local example could be duplicated nationwide.

At the same time, there were some constructive things happening. Civil rights, especially the affirmative action clause, opened new doors for the advancement of educated and/or skilled blacks. Employment opportunities multiplied. Blacks no longer were limited to occupations or professions that had been traditionally open to them. Consequently, the relative prestige, economic benefits, and other advantages of the teacher in the black schools diminished. We need only mention the opportunities now available in business administration in the computer age to illustrate this point. Computer skills can be acquired within a few months after high school by the gifted black youngster. Someone with a good grasp of math and science can bypass the humanities and move forward rapidly in financial gain and social betterment. Whereas education, ministry, medicine, and law had been avenues open for blacks, mainly to serve their own people, the computer opened up opportunities in the larger society. There was also the advantage of instant success and gratification for those unwilling or unable to pursue the long and expensive educational process.

There is also a downside to this new trend. This new situation that provided advancement in the business world for blacks often led to their alienation from the black community. Contacts with nonblacks led some

The Prophethood of Black Believers

young people to forget or even ignore their own roots and family values. Blacks now gave themselves over to the corporations that hired them. They often moved into integrated neighborhoods. They and their children lost contact with their own people as well as institutions in the black community. Many of them turned away from black colleges and sent their children to Ivy League colleges to be schooled in Euro-American knowledge. The result is a new breed of black intellectuals with a serious identity crisis. Several of the neoconservatives used by the Republican administrations to work against programs of uplift for all black people have come from this group. We are paying the price for these new opportunities. We have fewer strong, dedicated leaders for racial uplift. For as these new intellectuals become color-blind, blacks in the underclass are being abandoned, with few to really care about or understand their plight or needs. Again the black church and black pastor have an urgent challenge.

Ministry to those well-educated youth and young adults is a great burden to many black pastors. Too many black pastors are themselves inadequately educated for leadership of the black middle class. Unfortunately, most American seminaries are not preparing black theological students to cope with the type of educational ministry outlined in this study. As a theological educator and theologian for many years, I am speaking from both data and observation. While some black seminaries are attempting to address these needs, most white seminaries are educating black students for a ministry and mission that does not exist except in a few integrated churches.

The loss of the humanities and fine arts in the education of youth for the computer age leaves much to be desired in addressing the total person and the whole human situation. Black churches need to see clearly their new task for ministry to a new generation.

Summary

The problems addressed in this chapter reflect a grave concern for value clarification for black people, especially the young, through Christian education. Traditionally, preaching has been central to the black church tradition. While I trust that we will continue to excel in preaching with both fervor and teaching content, education in the moral and spiritual values of the Christian faith will be greatly needed. We must lift up the rich content of our African heritage to give our people a sense of worth as well. Only thus will we be able to save our generations. We must seek every opportunity to educate our congregations. A thorough program of education must be offered if we are to meet the needs of our people for spiritual insight and moral direction. Perhaps the most important assertion of this chapter is the need for the leadership of the black pastor as educator. As the leader of the congregation, the pastor determines the quality of the educational ministry of black churches.

5

Faith Development and Ministry to Black Youth

IN THE DISCUSSION OF "EDUCATION MINISTRY" IN THE previous chapter we were concerned generally with the education of the entire church membership. Here we will focus our attention upon youth.

Black churches now have the main responsibility for teaching moral values. We can no longer consider families to be the principal "moral school for children." We need to teach personal and social ethics based upon broad-based knowledge. Biblical and theological ethics are foundational, but wide sources of knowledge are necessary. The goal is to make life more human on all fronts.

Nature and Nurture: Principles of Youth Development

The perspective on "faith development" as outlined by James Fowler can be useful if not conclusive for our teaching ministry, especially with youth.[1] Much that he assumes is based upon careful research in the field of educational psychology, in which various theories of development have been subject to rigorous tests. In addition, Fowler has brought religious and ethical insights to bear upon his impressive research. The work of many original scholars undergirds Fowler's creative project, including Lawrence Kohlberg, Jean Piaget, Erik Erikson, Emile Durkheim, William James, and John Dewey. These and other influences upon Fowler are mostly humanistic in orientation. While they emphasize the moral dimension, Fowler strongly emphasizes the faith dimension as well.

In his emphasis upon faith in his project, Fowler recalls, for me, the important contribution Horace Bushnell made to theology by way of

55

Christian education. There are two reasons why I am moved by what Fowler offers: first, and most important, he shares my theological interest. He is very much a theologian of the church. Second, he focuses on "nurture" in education. This gets us beyond any assertion that blacks or other minorities are "naturally" inferior. It is important to launch our discussion with the assumption that growth in moral and religious values transcends racial or cultural differences. Only thus may we tackle vigorously the educative task of our churches among youth.

We are able to learn much from educational psychology and faith development for our youth ministry. There are several positive assumptions: (1) Nurture is at least as important as nature (genetic transmission of traits of character). (2) What happens in the early years of a child's life makes a lasting impression on development or growth (emotional and moral-religious). (3) The social environment has a powerful impact upon the future direction of one's life. (4) How we understand and relate to stages of growth (or development) has a significant impact upon maturation and learning patterns. On the whole, we know that socialization and value clarification are essential to human development in a wholesome direction. When there is wanton neglect of these matters, humans do not grow into the best examples of mature adults. This outlook based on faith development sets a large agenda for black churches in their ministry to youth.

Complementarity of Family and Church in the Black Tradition

There are many positive programs for black youth in public and private schools. However, this is true not so much because these institutions are geared for this task but because of dedicated teachers and principals in the schools. Even so, our concerted and orchestrated efforts must be in the home and the church.

We must hold a realistic view of black family strength. In reaction to severe criticism of the weakness of black families, some of our leaders have turned to romantic and sentimental praise of black families. Taking into account how slavery and racism have dealt devastating blows to the black family, we must judge our family situation with sober realism if we are to move progressively forward. Urbanization and the drug epidemic are the most recent and decisive enemies of black family health. All the foes of black family strength must be confronted and overcome if we are to save our generations.

Again, we must no longer look for the ideal family—a husband, wife, and children—as the only model of black family life. Although we must find ways to lift up and celebrate that ideal, we must not neglect or look down upon other models of family life. In our ministry to black people we must welcome and seek to enrich all families. Many of our families will consist of single-parent households. Most often the parent will be a teenage girl or a woman. Usually children are involved and they must be nurtured and cared for if they are to become wholesome adult persons. All families should find encouragement, empowerment, and enrichment in the black church.

It will be helpful if we can begin to see all families as part of a kinship network. Whereas the single-parent family gains most from this outlook, all families need the support of a larger kinship group. It is good for parents and children to sense that they belong to a large sharing and caring kinship network that is intergenerational. Today many mature and responsible adults attribute much of their success to grandparents, aunts, and uncles. The extended family is part of our African heritage that needs now to be reclaimed and celebrated. The black family reunion movement is part of this august past. Black churches need to encourage consciously and openly this revival of emphasis on the extended family. It can be turned to constructive use for the empowerment of black families. A generation of healthy and whole young people may well be the result of the effort.

The black churches also need to define themselves as extended families. There are biblical and theological warrants for this self-understanding of the church. In the Old Testament, Israel is often conceived of as a "corporate personality," the people of God. This is likewise true of the church. The church is referred to as the family of God or the household of faith. Even the model of the church as the "body of Christ" speaks to "unity-in-diversity." The extended family is one in which everybody counts and belongs. The oppressed, the downtrodden, the outcast, the homeless need to look to the black church as their extended family. This outlook is in keeping with the ministry of Jesus, the lord of the church. It represents his concern for the downtrodden, the confused, the oppressed. Beyond this the black church has a noble heritage of *ujamaa*, "familyhood," deeply rooted in the African notion of caring and sharing. It is couched in the maxim: "because I am, we are." We as black people need to take seriously this background of faith and heritage as we view the church as an extended family.

Indeed, the roles of family and church as extended entities are complementary. However, it is through our ministries in the church that the interfacing activities between church and family must take place. Black churches must provide the knowledge, inspiration, and often the means to lift up families. Churches are to provide the programs and offer the space to enrich black families. In a word, leadership must come from the churches if our families are to regain their place as "moral schools for children." Churches and families have separate roles in nurturing the young. Together they can do much to alter the present crisis in family life.

The Status of Black Children and Youth

It is alarming to observe and study the plight for our young. Poverty is rampant in our rich country, and the major victims are children—our future. Children did not ask to be born. Until they are of voting age, they have no political self-determination. They are dependent upon the love and concern of empowered adults. Too many adults in our society are obsessed with greed and selfishness. Children are the poorest of the poor, the oppressed of the oppressed. Yet, without their development into mature and responsible adults, our nation has no future.

The situation among black children appears to be worst of all. It is devastating to be young, black, and poor in America. Marian Wright Edelman, who heads the Children's Defense Fund, recently provided a comprehensive report on children in America.[2] This report is must reading for all who care about the plight of America's children. The seriousness of the plight of black children is highlighted when we realize that although black people constitute about 10 percent of the total population, 35 out of every 100 poor children in America are black. In that 54 out of every 100 children in America live in female-headed families, the number of black children living in a female-headed family is high indeed. The high incidence of teenage pregnancy and the feminization of poverty create a devastating situation of poverty for black children. This information is important for black church leaders. The socioeconomic as well as the political situation has a lot to do with the shape of our ministry.

Many urban black pastors report that they face a new type of ministry to black youth. Neither their previous experience nor their theological education prepared them for ministry to black underclass youth. These young people are educated on the street. They have no knowledge of real family, have no acquaintance with the church, and have never been employed. They are almost completely outside the "system." The street is their only known institution. They are streetwise and skilled in the means of survival on the mean streets of our urban ghettos. Many enter the drug culture, prostitution, and other illegal activities. The only family they know is the gang that they join for both survival and protection. They soon are caught up in a cult of violence that devalues all human life and property. Socialization into the gang or peer group often involves pressures against membership in any mainstream institution.

The Prophethood of Black Believers

Black churches are especially rejected as the province of older and "straight" types.[3]

Ministering to underclass black youth is a real challenge. First of all, the minister needs to be aware of the existence of this group of young people. He or she must enter their world. This world can be approached through studies, particularly social science studies. Some educational studies are also invaluable. However, studies are not the end of ministry; they are only a means. There must follow a deep sense of caring for underclass youth. One has to find a means of encounter in the life-world of these young people. There are no traditional approaches to these youth. Yet some pastors have been effective in working with underclass youth. Personal discovery and models of ministry found to be effective elsewhere must serve as the minister's guide.

Eric Lincoln found a lack of concern for youth ministry in his study of the black church. Ministry to adults tended to dominate most church programs. Programs for youth ranked low on the agenda of many pastors of black churches.[4] This outlook of black clergy is shortsighted. Without youth, churches have a short future. And the church is always in need of the vitality of youth. Leadership for the future of the church must be recruited from the ranks of young people.

Lincoln observes that most of the programs designed to attract black youth to the church are traditional. These programs include youth choirs, youth groups, evangelistic programs, Bible study, and recreational and social events. He is correct in pointing out that these traditional approaches leave untouched the major concerns of the underclass black youth. Among these are the racial identity crisis, unemployment, prison confinement of many black youth, teenage motherhood, and the drug culture.[5] In other words, most ministries to black youth, especially to the underclass, have not entered the living world of those persons whose lives we seek to change. Bible study or evangelistic activity that does not enter that world is likely to be ineffective.

The Black Church and the Self-Help Tradition

Self-help is being lifted up as a principle of salvation for black people. A close look at the state of many black people raises questions about this "bootstrap" ideology. How does one motivate hopeless people? To what does one appeal? So many have dropped out of society and out of life itself because of the oppression they have felt in that society. In the absence of role models or mentors, where does one begin?

Leon Sullivan, an athlete in his youth, picked up a basketball and played with boys of the streets of Philadelphia. He won their confidence.

Soon they were in Sunday school and church. Several of the young men excelled in vocations and professions. Beyond his church ministry, he founded Opportunities Industrialization Centers. OIC is now both national and international. At first, it was funded by members of the Zion Baptist Church of Philadelphia. It started in an old jailhouse. In Sullivan's own words, "a house of despair was turned into a house of hope." Sullivan soon discovered two things: one has to be motivated to improve one's life and one has to procure employment after one has developed one's skills. His ministry, therefore, involved such methods as boycotts and other forms of nonviolent economic, social, and political action. For more than three decades, however, the base for his ministry was the pastorate of the Zion Baptist Church.

His prior work with youth as assistant to Adam Clayton Powell, Jr., and as a staff person of the mayor of New York City prepared Sullivan for his ministry to youth in Philadelphia. This unique ministry to youth is only one sterling example of an intervention in a situation of youth in crisis. It also indicates that self-help for the oppressed has to be supported by institutional efforts to bring about change. Because of this need for institutional support, the affirmative action project of the American government should not have been cut off when it was just beginning to uplift a few blacks. If slavery, the ultimate dehumanization of blacks, could last for several centuries, the project of uplift should have lasted much longer than it did. This need for systemic change is the reason black churches are solidly for aggressive civil rights for black people. Again, our youth have most to gain from such an approach.

It is in the black church—with its cross section of membership, with its "haves" and "have-nots," with its educated and uneducated, all worshiping and associating as an extended family—that the black underclass youth can find a sense of worth and belonging.[6] Those who study the black underclass point to the social isolation of black youth from the black working class as well as the black middle class. The social contacts of different economic groups once available in the cohesive black community have been cut off. Jobs have left the central cities and with them black workers and professional people have disappeared. Underclass youth need role models. Otherwise, what they see is all they know. Black churches are in a unique position to overcome this isolation and provide important role models for young people who are not acquainted with the values of the black self-help tradition. Preaching and teaching self-help needs to be reinforced by role models of working adults. The church is a place where black self-help values can be internalized in a loving and caring environment. Eric Lincoln uses the Church of God in Christ as a prime example of the black self-help tradition. This denomination began as a host of illiterate, poor, rural migrants in urban centers. It now has a significant number of middle- and working-class black members. The fact that it is the fastest growing black denomination in the ghettos of our country should say something about the effectiveness it has in its ministry to the black underclass.

We are speaking here of a subculture of survival. In a real sense blacks have never been fully admitted into mainstream American culture. This is true even of those who have striven to be fully qualified. It is not surprising that poor blacks are woefully disadvantaged and underrepresented. The members of the black underclass are trapped in neighborhoods and crowded substandard housing complexes and subject to abject poverty. Women are often third-generation welfare recipients. There are too many cases where the grandmother, mother, and daughter have children by multiple fathers and there is no responsible male role model available. In the past the grandfather or uncle in the extended family embodied the character of a responsible, mature male. Thus, children of both sexes learned to appreciate the importance of the adult male for family health. This new family situation makes the adult male expendable and even undesirable. Too many black girls see the male as serving only a procreative role. This outlook is now reaching a disastrous dimension.

If girls see the birthing of children without male companionship and love as normative, boys see girls as a means to temporary sexual gratification. Too many black males see no merit or fulfillment in fatherhood. As a father and grandfather, I find it difficult to understand this. But the present custom is to sire children with no bonding or love involved. Unemployment and lack of economic means must be considered. Even after one blames the welfare system and unemployment, one still needs a better explanation for what has happened to responsible manhood among young black males. It is obvious that we have lost something that is essential to black family life. Without responsible fatherhood, we have a dark destiny as a people.

Lack of economic means and racism do not constitute a total answer to the question of why this problem exists. Something tragic has happened to black family life in our urban and rural areas. Even during slavery we have accounts of strong ties between fathers and their children. Many of us knew abject poverty, but we were nurtured on the love of our parents. The love that bonds parent to child overcomes the devastating effects caused by adverse circumstances. If one has a *why* for living, he or she can overcome just about any *how*! I submit that this is where black churches can provide vital resources for black family empowerment. Faith is not a substitute for knowledge and know-how, but it is a powerful motivator for the type of self-help and self-direction we need to reclaim our families.

Ministry to Black Middle-Class Youth

Ministry to black middle-class young people presents its own challenge. Many such young people leave or ignore the black church. They present a unique and important task for ministry in black churches. If the black churches are to pursue an effective ministry to all black people, they must reclaim this sizable number of gifted and intelligent black youth. They must do so for two reasons: for the youth themselves and their own future as Christians, and for these young people to serve as workers to uplift others who are less fortunate. Some of these young people who are doing well in their educational preparation are emerging into the middle class from the ranks of the black poor. Some are children of single-parent families. These latter youth need to be a part of peer groups in the church fellowship for support and continual growth.

It is a fact that many pastors are uneducated or undereducated. Certainly, ministry is a divine calling and some black ministers are doing an exceptional job in total ministry without formal college or seminary education. In the final analysis ministry is a spiritual gift. However, proper study and formal education can lead to a significant enrichment and empowerment of whatever natural talents a minister has. We should prepare to give God our best in ministry. This requires serious and continual study. The study of the Bible is essential, but there is a further requirement that we be prepared to interpret and apply the biblical message to the needs of our generation, including the young.

Ministry to black middle-class young people, including young adults, is a real test of our preparation for ministry, insofar as our formal education is concerned. Young people who have experienced high school and higher education have disciplined their minds to think and analyze issues. When the minister speaks or preaches, they carefully observe his or her diction and the trend of thought. We would be naive to expect them to leave their heads outside the sanctuary. Thus, they are best challenged by a minister who is well prepared in the use of language as well as thought. This implies years of formal education. To know the issues requires constant study and observation.

Theological education should be a *plus* and not a *minus*. Education for ministry does not preclude the fundamentals of ministry—a divine call and a sensitivity for the needs of God's people, within and outside of the congregation. Even a well-educated minister must have a strong sense of servanthood in order to be effective as shepherd of a spiritual flock. He or she will need to be flexible and to use the know-how of research and reflection to establish rapport with middle-class black youth by entering their world. He or she will need to be understanding of the realities of that world and the powerful impact of peer pressure upon moral standards and spiritual values. A minister of any age needs to "revisit" his or her own youth as a basis for contact.

Once there is a fusion of horizons—the horizon of the minister and of the young people—a concrete plan of ministry to these youth must be developed. A pastor needs, for instance, to be aware of the intellectual ideologies and social aspects of the learning situation. She or he needs to be close to young people among friends or relatives, as well as to his or her own sons, daughters, or grandchildren. The more the minister enters the world of young people, the more he or she will be able to address the needs of these young people in programs and activities. There must be opportunities for young people to express themselves in words and deeds.

During the last two decades, due to the search for roots, black youth have been attracted by gospel music. It is not certain how deep their religious understanding has been or how constructive the response of ministers to this new influx of young black middle-class youth has been. A form of neopentecostalism seems attractive to these young people. It is not clear whether this super-emotionalism is from the presence of the Holy Spirit or a quest for African heritage. The matter requires serious study if we are to capture this new enthusiasm of middle-class black youth for constructive religious purposes. In the meantime, teaching, counseling, and other activities should be vigorously pursued with these young people. Worship as a whole, as well as most church programs, should involve the young people for the mutual growth and enrichment of all the people of God.

Summary

This discussion of ministry to youth is incomplete. Some salient concerns will be taken up in subsequent chapters. Here I have touched on the roles of nature and nurture in youth development. I must leave the question of genetics to those more prepared than I to discuss it. My focus has been on nurture. The social and psychological environment, together with familial and economic factors, have much to do with how young people develop into adulthood. Our ministries must take such factors into account. The work of James Fowler in faith development can be taken as a model. The complementary nature of the roles of family and church in the black tradition is a major concern of mine. Mutual aid societies and self-help issues are not new, since the black church has sponsored and nurtured these activities from its inception. We have only to build on this practice and update the application. Although most of my discussion in this chapter has centered on a concern for poor, black, urban youth, I closed with a concern for ministry to middle-class youth. Much of the potential for leadership for the uplift of all black people rests with this latter group. They must see their relationship to all black people. They must realize that they must not be co-opted nor separated from the black underclass. Unless all are free, none is free. It is the peculiar mission of the black church to make this important point obvious to black middle-class youth.

6

The Black Minister and Pastoral Care

AS A THEOLOGIAN, WITH A LIBERATIONIST CON-
sciousness out of the black heritage, I view pastoral care as *priestly*.
While this aspect of ministry is intertwined with the *prophetic* aspect, the
two aspects need separation for clarity of treatment.[1] The gospel is for
the whole person and for all people. There is a comforting, succoring dimension to the gospel as well as a disturbing message for personal and
societal evils. God speaks and acts in mercy as well as judgment. Here
we draw upon the Christian message that consoles and heals. Thus, for
me, pastoral care is priestly in outlook.

The Work of Edward P. Wimberly

The work of black theologians and pastors in the field of pastoral
care has been carefully researched and tested in various aspects of ministry, such as the pastorate or in counseling and therapy. Among the
most definitive studies are those by Edward P. Wimberly. In his first,
landmark volume, *Pastoral Care in the Black Church*,[2] Wimberly lays a
good groundwork for his future reflections. He sees the black minister
primarily as one who sustains and guides his or her people. He also emphasizes family enrichment. The most useful aspect of his concern for
family health is his stress upon the "sub-systems" in the family and how
these must be addressed if the entire family is to be healthy and whole.
For example, if there is serious tension between siblings, it may be reflected in husband-wife (father-mother) strife. If parental tensions get
all the attention, the real cause of the tension in the family remains.

In his latest book, *African American Pastoral Care*,[3] Wimberly presents the narrative or story-telling method of counseling in the black

church. He is aware of the strengths and weaknesses of this method commonly used by pastors and lay persons in the black church. On the downside, it can be too subjective, it can downgrade formal education for ministry, and it can become more pastor-focused than "counselee-parishioner centered." On the positive side, storytelling can facilitate growth and empathy and foster a care relationship between the pastor and the parishioner.[4] In this work as well as in his first major work, Wimberly stresses the principle of the "priesthood of all believers" in a congregation. The narrative tradition, he insists, is native to the black church tradition. Hence, it opens up the possibility of lay people helping and caring for each other.

Here Wimberly touches a nerve point in the black church. A particular role of the black theologian is to criticize the black church when doing so can be a constructive contribution. In the work *Pastoral Care in the Black Church*, Wimberly made certain observations about black pastors that are worth repeating here. He said that a black church fellowship is like an extended family. This can be good for all if it works. However, black pastors are often viewed as a father (or parent). If so, the vital question is, What kind of parent? If the parent is autocratic and leads through coercion, that leadership stifles the initiative and creativity of gifted and talented lay persons. It creates a forbidding climate of total dependence upon the pastor. This may increase his or her control and consolidate personal influence, but it can destroy the ability of lay persons to make their best contribution to the ministry of the church. I agree with Wimberly that, for all purposes of ministry, it is better to lead by example and persuasion than by coercion. This will free lay persons to care for and console one another. Since the narrative approach is already present, the pastor can help to refine this method of counseling so that members can be priests to one another.

The African American Healing Tradition

The care manifest in black churches did not begin on these shores. Care for one another, based upon blood or spiritual kinship, existed and continues to exist in several African countries, including West Africa, the ancestral home of most African Americans. In 1989, I observed this tradition in Soweto in South Africa while I was living with an African family. In my late evening conversations with the husband/father, I learned much about traditional African life. Much of that tradition was reflected in conversation and observations in West and East African countries as well.

Two examples must suffice to make the point. In the first instance my South African host told how he was able to build a substantial and comfortable home amid the slums of Soweto. He was an active member of a congregation where everyone mattered. Each member viewed the church as a family. Where there was need and a call for help, everyone who could help in any way would support the person in need. Therefore, when he decided to build his house, a contractor offered his time, knowledge, and resources, without the benefit of salary. Since real estate loans to build good quality housing are difficult for Africans to acquire, the reduced cost (mainly materials) made it possible for my friend to get the loan he needed to build a high-quality house for his family.

Another example occurred when, during my month's visit, a member of this church died. The family was too poor to handle the funeral expenses. My African host, together with other leaders in this congregation, gave and collected sufficient funds to bury the deceased. While such action appears to be merely a Christian response, the frequency and naturalness of this mutual aid type of response makes one ponder it deeply.

Albert Schweitzer, who generally gave little attention to the merits of African culture, used one African tradition to benefit his medical practice. He discovered a tradition among African healers of surrounding an ill person with family members to aid the recovery. Schweitzer, therefore, built traditional dwelling places in the vicinity of his hospital in Lambarane where family members could live while illnesses were being treated in the hospital he established. It was discovered that this custom greatly assisted his medical practice. He thus plugged into the African healing tradition and, at the same time, used the strong familial tradition to benefit his patients.

In the same spirit we recall that the first connectional black churches (for example, the African Methodist Episcopal) grew out of mutual aid societies. Mutual aid organizations were designed by blacks to help one another out of a sense of kinship. The fact that the leadership in Philadelphia was ministerial—for example, that of Richard Allen—tied this self-help movement immediately to the birth of a new denomination. However, the impulse itself was well established in the roots of black history and culture, with African precedents.

In a similar manner, the present black family reunion movement is based upon the black heritage with African roots. It involves much more than the genealogical research going on in the larger society. It is related to a need to survive as an oppressed group. Alex Haley's *Roots* gave real zest to the black family reunion movement because it connected the Afro-American past with African roots. It seems to me, however, that the movement really speaks to the need for self-help and self-determination in a hostile environment—for individuals and for peoples. Self-help, peoplehood, mutual aid with a dose of black consciousness and religious commitment, all converge in the black family reunion movement. The church connection and the intergenerational outreach of the black family reunion movement make it very important for survival and constructive growth toward the future. Black pastors need to enter vigorously into this movement to give it direction. There is a need to give careful study to the family reunion among blacks to provide constructive leadership. Black church fellowship and worship can deeply enrich and empower the black family reunion movement.

My own experience is a case in point. As a boy of sixteen I graduated from high school as valedictorian. The following autumn I entered college away from home. Because I left home for study so early, I never came to know members of my blood kinship network. During several years of advanced study I only infrequently visited my parents and two sisters. In the custom of the black family and church tradition, I was adopted everywhere I went by black couples, especially in the church. Sometimes I was "adopted" by ministerial couples and often by lay couples. Always I had a family that claimed me and a place I could call home in the black church and community. This was true in Hartford, Connecticut, where I lived during the weekdays on the campus. On weekends I lived in a home in the black community. At first, I lived with my senior pastor and his wife. Soon a childless deacon couple invited me into their home as a son. This process continued until I married and started my own family. These kinship relations, though bloodless, meant much and explain my intense interest in family enrichment and empowerment. All young people need the nurture and belongingness of family for healthy growth into mature and responsible adults. My early call to the ministry enhanced my personal experience.

When I married, I united with a large extended family. From the beginning of this union I was accepted as a son. All the relatives of my wife became my kin. We found this extended family acceptance so important that we decided to make sure that our children would become a part of a larger family network. This was not easy when we moved to Washington, D.C., while the extended family remained in North Carolina. The association with the larger family was so important to us, however, that we used every opportunity to be with the family in North Carolina or to have them visit us. During the last decade this process has been sustained by an annual family reunion with an attendance of 150 to 200 relatives from all over the United States.

The most sobering aspect of our family reunion is the awareness of the depleting ranks of older persons claimed by death. The most exhilarating result has been the attendance and full participation of the new generations of young people. First our children and now our grandchildren are a part of it. A nephew who is under thirty is convener. Activities fully claim the enthusiastic involvement of people of all ages. There is a wholesome interaction and sharing by all. This reunion includes a religious component in the formal program and ends with Sunday worship in a local church. While any human endeavor has behind-the-scenes problems and complaints, this growth of the family reunion movement among blacks is generally positive. It can mean much for the health of black people through the strengthening of black family life. It is one important way to nurture the young.

Intervention in a Spiral of Violence

The cult of violence that reigns in our major cities seems to go beyond even the influence of drugs. Violence seems to be the order of the day. It is obvious that drug-related crime is on the upward swing, but there seems to be a deeper psychological and spiritual infection in our society, especially among black youth. Senseless and brutal homicide among young black males has reached epidemic dimensions. All caring persons need to be concerned with the *why* of this internal genocide. Not only is there danger that black males will wipe each other out, but also there is a societal problem of major proportions. No one and no area of our metropolitan centers is safe or secure. It is time for all Americans to become concerned.

In the meantime, the major white denominations express concern about sexuality (especially abortion and homosexuality), with some attention given to health care. White women are concerned about inclusive language and how to overcome dependency upon white men. A black female pastor in the United Methodist Church told me that in the marriage ceremony of that church, the father no longer "gives the bride away." This minister and I reflected upon how this concern is meaningless to most black women, who are proud to have a present and caring father at their wedding. It also illustrates that in predominantly white denominations blacks go along with decisions while their own priorities are low on the official agenda or most often absent. As long as this is so, there will be a crying need for black denominations.

Ministry in the inner cities of America is in the midst of violence. In some cases, the streets are as dangerous as jungles infested with wild beasts of prey. Human beings are killing each other without any regard for the sacredness of human life. There is the absence of conscience or the regard for the right of another to exist. Life is considered valueless and expendable. Being at the wrong place at the wrong time can be fatal. This situation has been developing for a long time, but with the infestation of drugs we now face an epidemic. Violence is present in the environment of too many black youth, with all its rawness and brutality.

Our streets are like a battlefield where some believe they have only the options of killing or being killed. Many black males have concluded that they will not live to be thirty.

All young people face the difficult personal and social decisions that go with the transition from childhood to adulthood. While the primary cause of death among black males is homicide, suicide is more often the cause of death among white males. While there appear to be more teenage pregnancies among black females, this does not necessarily indicate that they are more sexually permissive than white females of the same group. Here we seem to be dealing with percentages rather than persons, but understanding these youths in their social-racial contexts is crucial for ministry.

This concern spills over into middle-class homes and communities. For example, black males must choose very carefully their friends, male and female, or they are easily drawn into the culture of violence. A poor choice can mean, if not sudden death, a long prison term. The police as well as those who administer justice are rarely kind to any black youth. There seems to be a plan to incarcerate or destroy by any means the present generation of black males. The presence of major prisons, not only jails but penitentiaries, in the heart of the inner cities sends a message to black youth that is self-destructive.

While we cannot discuss fully this issue of violence here, it is important to keep in mind as we consider pastoral care in relation to ministry in the black church. There needs to be real concern for the cause and cure of violence so destructive to black people.

Mayor Sharon Pratt Kelly of Washington, D.C., finds herself immersed in a violent situation. She is struggling to find some of the answers. Police power and stricter sentences will not stop violence if people no longer care about life as such. Thus, she is now asking deeper questions. She has reflected on the breakdown of family life and the lack of male presence in the home. Young men are growing up without discipline and with no sense of values. We could add two complicating factors to this list of things that are missing in the life of young people in inner cities: Youth are often without education and without jobs (legitimate jobs). When there is a void, something else comes in to fill it. These young people are educated and socialized on the street. They view television many hours daily. Television that features wanton violence and perverse views of human sexuality appeals to the basest aspects of human nature. Sex is presented often as a violent act, and even "the good guys" triumph through violence. Our culture is violent. Even our nation settles its disputes through cataclysmic violence, as in Desert Storm.

As a director of the Albert Schweitzer Fellowship, I was made aware of the pain we caused the Iraqi people. Most of our attacks were from the air. Our pilots, who were technicians of death, did not need to deal with the human pain resulting from their attacks. They could return to their base with glee. To the American people they were heroes. The God-and-country syndrome brought out the worst in our American psyche. Nevertheless, a few Americans really cared about the pain and death of innocent people. I was moved by the concern of some physicians who share Schweitzer's "reverence for life" principle. They spoke of the suffering, disease, and deaths in the wake of Desert Storm. Thus, while many "righteous" people rejoiced over the victory we sustained in the name of God, these physicians, some of whom were not Christians, bemoaned the human cost. The tendency to see violence as a panacea filters down to our young. When circumstances seem hopeless, they may buy into violence as a way to survive. In some cases violence seems to bring their only fulfillment.

Our ministry, therefore, must seek to provide an alternative to violence. A small beginning would be to teach the very young nonviolent ways to resolve conflict. Here the Oriental arts of self-defense could be useful. Some of these martial arts encompass exalted spiritual, humanistic, and ethical values. In our own Judeo-Christian tradition, there is much to be lifted up in the Ten Commandments, in respect for life and love of others. As blacks we can draw upon the African sense of community and the strong extended family tradition. This African tradition has respect for elders and includes rites of passage that socialize young people in important values.

Finally, I would recommend more dissemination of the teachings of nonviolence by Dr. Martin Luther King Jr. There are writings about King's life and work suitable for children, teenagers, and young adults. In keeping with Wimberly's use of narrative in counseling, creative use of stories of the life and work of people like Gandhi, King, Rosa Parks, and others could begin to provide another perspective. Forgiveness and reconciliation should replace the focus on revenge and death.

An example comes to mind from my visit to South Africa. I hesitate to report negatively on the Zulu people in view of the deadly tension between Zulu Inkatha and the African National Congress (ANC). Also, because reporters have spent more time with the ANC, they reflect its perspective in their reports. However, recent revelation of government funding of Inkatha rallies supports much of the criticism of Zulu-inspired conflict. It was reported that Zulu culture is bent on revenge, even that Zulus kill the infant sons of their enemies. Since they believe in revenge they assume that everybody else does. Therefore, they destroy the "seed" of their enemies in order to insure that such revenge will not be possible. No society can exist if revenge and death are so central. In symbol, if not in fact, we seem to have in our culture of violence a revenge obsession. In our teaching, preaching, and counseling, we must seek a nonviolent alternative. Our faith provides that other way. We must give it hands and feet.

The Shepherding Role of the Black Pastor
Against the System

Pastoral care in the black church has to work against the power structures of oppression. The main concern of pastoral care is to comfort and heal, but this does not occur in a vacuum. Personal, familial, and societal forces interface. All these affect the healing experience. It seems cruel and bizarre to prosperous Americans that occasionally a black, poor mother abandons a child as an act of mercy. It does not occur to well-housed, well-fed people that a mother, of all people, could be driven to such a desperate act. Such a circumstance should prompt us to look at a hopeless person in the context of a system of oppression.

There are evil or mentally ill persons in all races and classes. The effects of drug addiction know no bounds. Many of the extreme situations, like the one just described, result from the terrible affliction of drug addiction. The abuse of alcohol must not be overlooked: too many young people, female and male, abuse alcohol for this problem to be denied. In the meantime, the oppression that comes to the black and poor people of this nation must be addressed. Otherwise we treat the results of oppression and overlook the oppressions themselves.

Several black pastors, as they reflected on the bicentennial, spoke of the system in the United States as a "trinity." This American trinity was capitalism, racism, and militarism.[5] There is an interconnection between the members of this trinity of oppressive forces. All have struck a decisive blow against the health and well-being of black people. In a real sense the black church is a force for systemic change. The pastor is in a position to spearhead the protest against injustices if she or he is informed and committed to liberation. People need to be taught that the Christian faith demands protest against injustices.

Often the first step toward liberation is psychological. Psychological liberation is a precondition for political freedom. Carter Woodson once observed that if a person's mind is enslaved you don't need to have a back door (traditionally required for blacks to use in entering or leaving white homes and businesses in the South). A person with an enslaved mind will create a back door out of necessity. Calvin B. Marshall III, speaks of the "Afro-Saxon mentality" of some black people. This is the psychological urge to be white, believing that white is normative and best in all things, whether it be beauty or standards of right and wrong. Unfortunately, this approach is true for many black Christians when it

The Prophethood of Black Believers

comes to biblical interpretation and theology. Marshall also observed what he called the "Syndrome of the Colonized." I have seen this characteristic full grown in Asia and Africa. According to Marshall, it exists among blacks in the United States as well. It exists where people accommodate to what is and do not believe change to be possible. It is the feeling that "I've been down so long, that down don't bother me anymore."[6]

A final syndrome described by Marshall is called the "slave mentality." This belief holds that one's inferior status has been divinely ordered. People with this belief are content to be "good, God-fearing, patriotic, colored servants."[7]

David D. Hurst calls for a pastoral response to these unhealthy psychological conditions:

> The system produces these psychological conditions in black people. . . .
> The restoration of wholeness for the race is in the hands of the black
> pastor and the black church. The Liberating Word must say to
> wounded black spirits: Sure, there is a mean person out there who has
> hurt you badly. . . . At the same time, the Liberating Word should say
> that healing is not in imitating that person or thinking like that person
> or worshipping that person. Healing occurs when the cause of our disease is diagnosed and treated.[8]

The antidote is what Wayne Oates calls "the prophetic principle of face-to-faceness."[9] This is where the estrangement is engaged and the dehumanizing effects of the system give way to healing and wholeness. I call it "liberation and reconciliation" between equal persons under God.

Summary

We are to be ever aware that when it comes to holistic ministry, the priestly and prophetic aspects of ministry interface. But separation is needed in this discussion for the sake of emphasis. This chapter focused on the priestly aspects of ministry. At the outset I lifted up the unique contribution of Edward Wimberly, whose work has made a great impact upon the knowledge of pastoral care among African Americans. His work extends my own observations about the black family. I have attempted here to treat the healing experience from the African and Afro-American religious tradition as well as from my own experience.

Much of the experience of black youth is self-destructive and rooted in violence. Pastoral care must seek to intervene in this culture of violence. We must seek to forge a path through this tragic situation to health, sanity, and wholeness. Pastoral care in the black church must take on this challenge. The methods of Dr. Martin Luther King Jr. offer some suggestions for the nonviolent resolution of conflicts. His message was his life. Therefore, his life's work could be a powerful case study for all ages. Forgiveness and reconciliation must replace this trend toward revenge and death.

The black pastor, in opposing the system of oppression, must know that the system has a powerful impact on the plight of black people. Changing the system, therefore, is a challenge to the black pastor and church. The goal is the health and wholeness of black people.

Black churches need to stop copying white churches and denominations. They need to look at their own reality and set their own agenda. Black churches need to come out of the closet on topics that have been taboo. Things are too serious now for ministers to hesitate to speak out on issues of life and death. We need to seek the best information and resources for help. Reading and interpreting scripture for its own sake is not enough. We face new situations. We need to know the *what* and the *why* of these new situations. Since the Bible does not provide a "blueprint" for all situations, we must be prepared to use all the knowledge and experience available for decision and action. The horizon of the biblical message needs to make contact with the horizon in which decision and action must take place. All is to be under the guidance of the Spirit as we confront concrete problems. We must remember that our ministry is to be carved out through prayer as well as the power of God's Spirit. These are powerful resources of grace.

The Prophethood of Black Believers

7

Black Women and Ministry

THE BLACK CHURCH THRIVES ON THE ACTIVE PAR-
ticipation of black women. Most black churches would not survive apart
from the involvement of women. In fact, most black male ministers
would not accept leadership in a church that did not have a good percentage of women in the membership.

While women are expected to do the work of the church, men are the
acknowledged power brokers in the church. Although I am able to
speak with more authority regarding the black Baptist denomination,
the situation in other black denominations appears to be similar to that
of the Baptists, insofar as the leadership role of women is concerned. We
may begin with the assumption that women have difficulty acquiring
top leadership roles in most black denominations. The recent study by C.
Eric Lincoln and Lawrence Mamiya bears this out.[1]

The real crisis for women comes at the level of ordained ministry.
Baptists and the Church of God in Christ are generally opposed to
women as ordained ministers, particularly in the pastorate. The Progressive Baptist Convention appears to be moving faster than other Baptist
bodies toward the full certification and acceptance of women as full-
fledged ministers. The three black Methodist denominations—the
African Methodist Episcopal, the Christian Methodist Episcopal, and the
African Methodist Episcopal Zion Churches—have a better score than
other black denominations in the elevation of women to the pulpit.
Nonetheless, the absence of women in the bishopric, among general offi-
cers, and in major pastorates of these latter denominations raises serious
questions regarding any major breakthroughs in black Methodist ranks.
One needs to listen attentively, as well, to the candid reports of women
ministers who serve these denominations.

Nonetheless, in Baptist denominations, an increasing number of
women are full pastors or assistant pastors in major black Baptist

churches. Thus, progress is being made, but for women it is slow and painful.

It is worth mentioning that the deacon board of most black churches seems to be "the last frontier" of male domination. Very few black Baptist churches have attempted to bring women onto the board of deacons. This is true even when women serve well on the board of trustees or even as an ordained representative on the ministerial staff. We can thus assume that discrimination against women is a major problem in black denominations in general, and among black Baptists, in particular. Thus, the black theologian has the task of internal prophecy. He or she is duty bound to attack sexism in the black church. We now turn to this task.

A New Challenge for Black Churches

During the fifties and sixties women in seminaries, for the most part, prepared to be educators, missionaries, or evangelists. Often these women married ministers and became partners in ministry as they supported the ministry of their male spouse. Beginning in the seventies and escalating to full force in the eighties, women seminarians chose ordination and full ministerial leadership as their goal.

As teacher of many black women, I can attest to the firm conviction many of these women have regarding a divine call. I am aware of their personal sacrifice, courage, and devotion to the ministry. It has been my task to counsel, encourage, and support the efforts of these black women against many odds, personal and institutional. I have found many women to be able students and gifted servants of the church. Some have been very effective ministers once they have broken through barriers set up by male leadership in the churches.

Many black Baptist pastors have not studied at a seminary. Too many male ministers have not paid their academic dues. They are not, therefore, impressed by the large number of female students who are enrolled in theological studies preparing for ordained ministry at the highest level. To teach these sisters, to know them by name, and yet be aware of the terrible trials ahead when they encounter these entrenched male ministers, is indeed painful. One former student, who is a successful pastor in a large city, told me that black male ministers were organizing in her city to slow down the progress of black women in ministry, and that black male ministers were not required to study or work as hard as the women. Therefore, women had to give more effort in study and to their struggle. It is indeed unfortunate that black male ministers, victims of racist oppression themselves, should visit such oppression upon their sisters in ministry.

Thus we are facing a new phenomenon—the large influx of divinely called, well-educated, and talented black women in ministry. These women seek ordination and leadership at the highest level in our churches and denominations. I do not see how black male ministers will much longer be able to deny their claims to *bona fide* ministerial leadership. This situation is not merely an embarrassment. It is one of the major *sins* of black male leadership in the church. For this sin, we need repentance and forgiveness.

The Bible as a Stumbling Block

Just as in the case of racism, the Bible, which can set us free, also can be used to enslave. Biblical literalism is a convenient tool. It allows us to pick and choose passages that underwrite what we already have decided. Those male ministers who have already decided that women have a subordinate place in the home, society, and church, look for passages of scripture that seem to say exactly what they find necessary for the subjugation of women. They then use these passages to deny women their rightful place in ministry.

A sound procedure in biblical interpretation is to ask what a particular passage meant. Finding the answer will require a reconstruction of the historical and cultural context that gave rise to the passage in question. Once we have discerned the original message, then we should bring the message forward and ask what it means today, given a present context of meaning and decision. It is a fact that most ancient cultures were male dominated, as is, in fact, much of the third world today. But is this the divine intention? Is not partnership between men and women more consistent with the best reading of scripture? Subjugation of women makes it possible, even plausible, to keep women in a state of dependency. This denies their co-humanity. It is a rejection of the image of God present in females and males alike.

The Bible, then, can be a means to liberation or it can be an instrument of oppression. It is interesting that so many who speak of the guidance of the Spirit impose their own limits on the Spirit's expression. Any close observer of the quality and effectiveness of many black women in ministry could see the Spirit's working in their lives and ministries. Who are we finite, mortal males to determine the scope of the Spirit's witness in the church? If "even the rocks cry out," why not fellow human beings who happen to be females? Could it now be that God is doing a new thing in our midst? We ought to be open to this possibility, especially in view of the number and quality of women who are convinced that God has called them to the vocation of ordained ministry in the church of

Jesus Christ. Black male ministers cannot withstand God's intention. God's will *will* prevail!

Theological Reflection on Sexism in the Black Church

Any attempt to understand sexist oppression in the black community needs to be seen against the background of our African ancestry and the long history of oppression in the United States. Africans strongly emphasize physical generation and extended family. African family style is both communal and intergenerational. A relational quality of significance between the sexes exists in Afro cultures. A very high value is ascribed to children in the family. Even in the United States, black children have usually been informally adopted when no blood parents were available or if they were irresponsible. This concern for families and the welfare of children has been based in the black church.

Yet we must come to terms with the negative effects of racism upon black people, on women, men, and children. We are not here concerned about who got the worst breaks, women or men, during the long history of slave oppression, followed by continual discrimination. The magnitude of collective evil against black people is enormous, almost indescribable. We must now focus our attention and effort upon the means to overcome the alienation we face together. This is the only path toward reconciliation between the sexes in the black church.

It is tragic that black men often respond to racism through violent attacks upon their women and children. They also copy too frequently the worst practices of white men as they exploit women as objects of carnal pleasure and monetary gain, rather than respecting their status as equally dignified human beings. The result is devastating for black families as a whole. Black men, as a result of low self-esteem, which is in turn often related to lack of education, job skills, or employment, find themselves incapable of profound love and caring for women and children. What I call "the quest for mutuality" between black women and men demands that a whole set of problems be addressed. In many of my writings I have tackled "racism" as a theological task. Here I turn my attention to "sexism," especially in the black church. Although my proposals here are tentative, permit me to make some observations.

First, we need a fresh way of thinking. We need to forge an epistemological foundation for a common experience between black men and women. Holistic thinking emerges naturally out of our African roots. This African outlook can be enriched by biblical faith. I see here a threshold where black women and men may enter upon a mutual quest for wholesome relationships. The task should be viewed as educative, with considerable attention being given to youth. There is no reason why the problems we now face should be transmitted to the next generation. If our theology informs our life together, mutuality could be the fruit of our efforts for the black family and church.

African and African American thought is soulful or *affective*. This should not be contrasted, qualitatively, to intellectual or rational thought. It has cognitive content, but it includes feeling and intuition as well. Soulful thought challenges the mind, moves the heart, and claims the will. It is experienced in a holistic sense. Because it is *lived* thought, it aims at balance and harmony. Affective thinking is characteristic of blacks irrespective of gender. Theologically speaking, it has African roots and a biblical foundation.[2] We conclude that since all blacks, male and female, tend to think affectively, this could be useful in forging mutuality.

Second, there is a need to interpret the doctrine of sin in light of the fact of sexism in black churches. Like racism, sexism is a sin against creation. If God's creation is good, then any human outlook that opposes the divine intention is a manifestation of sin. Sexism is a sin against the divine purpose in the creation of humans, female as well as male. We affirm from the biblical accounts of creation an equality of all humans before God. The theological belief surrounding the *imago dei* lays the groundwork for this affirmation. The dignity of the human person is God-given and is not subject to human determination.

Any denial of the dignity and equality of persons in the divine creative act is a sin against creation. It is a form of self-glorification or idolatry. Humans who consider themselves as being superior to others because they are "male" seek, as it were, to become as gods. As creatures they would usurp the prerogatives of the Creator. This is the original pride, the cause of the first fall. This primeval fall can be reenacted; in fact, it is repeated whenever human beings indulge in exalting themselves to divine status. This we do when we seek to exalt ourselves above others, based upon false pride. Such pride can be conscious or unconscious. Its effects upon the oppressed are the same. Sexism, like racism, is a collective manifestation of evil. It is, therefore, often pre-conscious. It is subtle and difficult to detect and uproot. Overcoming sexism requires careful thought and decisive action, both personal and social.

This pride that caused the fall can be an indication of sexism as well as racism. Compare the use of the biblical account of Ham in reference to racism with the sexist interpretation of Eve as the first seductress. In the former instance, there is a misuse of a biblical text to support racism. In the latter case, there is a negative value ascribed to the body, especially that of females. Using the body-soul dichotomy, a disvalue is associated with human embodiment in the flesh. Sin and sexuality are brought together in such a way that women are viewed as temptresses who seduce men into acts of sexual sin. Eve becomes the original seductress, leading Adam to commit the original act of fornication. In this distorted exegesis we find a possible biblical grounding for sexism in the biblical texts of creation and fall.[3]

This distortion of biblical texts is all too familiar to those who are victims of racism. We recall how slave owners interpreted scripture to justify slavery. Added to the false exegesis of scripture was the use of dualism from Greek philosophy to theologize the misuse of scripture for the diabolical purpose of dehumanizing black people. We can thus see how both sexism and racism relate to faulty interpretations of the doctrine of creation. A theology of incarnational holism rooted in both African and biblical perspectives can offer much to offset false exegesis and theologizing, which undergird the two sins against creation. Black women are victimized by both sins. Therefore, it is important to discuss both in relation to each other.

A sin against creation arises, then, when human beings dare to challenge the divine purpose. God created an order and announced its goodness. When we reject the goodness of God's intentions in creation and attempt to re-order any aspect of it to enhance our self-ambition, we commit a sin against creation. In this context, then, sexism is a sin against creation. In the divine creative act, God made a distinction between males and females. This difference is obviously related to human love and pro-creation, to the family and the future of the human race. It is also related in some way to human involvement in the process of co-creation of both sexes. To consider women as unequal and to make of them mere objects of sexual pleasure and to deny them equal dignity is to belie God's creative plan. Sexism is a blatant example of a sin against creation.

Sexism is destructive of men as well as women, just as racism is destructive to the oppressor as well as the oppressed. It has often been observed that poor whites who sought to keep blacks down slowed their own uplift. The same can be said of men who invest so much time attempting to keep women in "their place." The argument that some women accept their bondage willingly only attests to their social and psychological conditioning; it does not make it right. If women accept the consequences of the sin of sexism, they face the loss of self-esteem.

Again, it is asserted that if women were free they would oppress men. This possibility does not justify the prior sin. We know this argument has been much used to sustain racist oppression. It must be rejected for it does not touch the ethical or theological core of the sin of sexism.

Women who accept the opinion of men that they deserve a lesser status than men often wallow in self-pity—they cannot be fulfilled as persons with equal worth and dignity. At the same time, men who consider themselves superior to women just because of their "maleness" are not

The Prophethood of Black Believers

able to affirm themselves. Often their lives are meaningless and without fulfillment. Such men may feel jealous and insecure as a result of any success realized by women. Though they may know many women as sexual partners, they may be incapable of profound love. The realization of the depths of the love-bond between women and men as equal partners eludes them. Sexism may induce illusions of inferiority in women and superiority in men. Both are counterproductive for self-realization and community. Sexism as a sin against creation requires repentance and forgiveness. Here as elsewhere "judgment begins at the house of God."

Sexism Is a Sin Against Grace

Carl Marbury, a New Testament scholar, offers support for the mutuality of men and women from his biblical reflections.[4] He refers to Jesus and Paul as providing a direction for us toward a wholesome equality between men and women. The black church is burdened by conflict in its unclear understanding of the appropriate arrangements for wholesome male-female relationships. Male leaders in the pulpit as well as in the pew are culpable. In this instance, an oppressed male-dominated church becomes an oppressing church in reference to women in the fellowship. It is urgent that considerable attention be given to explicating this problem. The issue is not whether black women accept an inferior status or role; it is, rather, whether they ought to lay claim to that which is theirs by God-given right as Christians who are equal to men in creation and through grace.

The issue of the rights of women to equal status and treatment is where theology and ethics, faith and practice meet. Here is a juncture where there is a clear theological grounding for ethics. Theology that addresses the quest for human freedom must inform our lives and all relationships as Christians. The major contribution of liberation theologies (including black and womanist versions) has been to analyze various forms of oppression (and the liberation from these oppressions) and to bring theology and ethics together in an inseparable bond. This has been the historic association of theology and ethics. Let us not be confused by labels.

If all have sinned and if all are equal in creation, then all are in need of the same grace to be set free from the consequences of sin. Men and women share equally in the condition of sinfulness. They are equally culpable, equally guilty, and, therefore, equally in need of repentance and forgiveness before God. All humans are saved by grace through faith. Salvation is ultimately a gift, though it does include human response and responsibility. In the final analysis all are saved by grace from God, who is creator of life and the redeemer of souls. Kneeling at the cross, men and women bear the same burden of need and are forgiven by the same grace. The source is God through Christ and by the agency of the Holy Spirit. Therefore, sexism is a sin against grace just as it is a sin against creation. The author of creation is also the giver of grace. Men as human beings do not have the right to interpose their wills over against God's purpose in creation or redemption.

Christian Baptism and the Quest for Mutuality

Christian baptism, according to Paul, implies a leveling of all distinctions, whether Jew or Greek, bond or free, male or female (Gal. 3:27–28). When one is baptized in Christ a oneness ensues that abolishes all such distinctions.

Again, Marbury points us to the Christian baptismal rite as a theological example that illustrates the mutuality between women and men. This specifically Christian understanding is in contrast to the Jewish rite of circumcision, which is avowedly sexist in that it is limited to males. Baptismal initiation is clearly open to men and women on the same basis and with the same meaning. (Correctives are now being made by Jews in regard to the sexist bias of the traditional rite.)

Baptism dramatically communicates the Christian's participation in the death and resurrection of Jesus Christ. It is the purification rite of the church that symbolizes the washing away of our sins and transgressions. Christians differ on the efficacy of the baptismal rite in reference to its regenerative purpose. They also have diverse interpretations regarding its proper administration. However, they are generally agreed that it is an essential rite of initiation into the family of God, the church.

This place of baptism in the Christian creed as well as in the worship and fellowship of the people of God makes it an example of considerable importance as we discuss the mutuality of women and men. It is a very helpful theological issue in support of our affirmation that the Christian faith is supportive of the mutuality of women and men. It is foundational to the claim that all are one in Christ Jesus. Baptism, therefore, complements our discussion on creation. It is associated with the experience of re-creation and undergirds the assertion that females and males are equals, whose difference is mutually complementary.

Sexuality, Spirituality, and Mutuality

Black Christian perspectives affirm the sanctity and wholeness of human life. Life is to be celebrated. Sexuality is a part of life. It is close to spirituality, embracing our total being. Sexuality is an aspect of all holistic affirmation of life, flesh as well as spirit. Sexuality is a part of a good creation. It is not to be separated from a total relationship between female and male. It does not belong to the Greek dichotomy of soul and body or the Puritan condemnation of the flesh as inherently evil.

There is some strange connection between the Puritan ethic and the hedonistic obsession and preoccupation with sex. When sex is viewed in its natural and holistic perspective as a part of the total life and a complete relationship between male and female, it takes on a healthy and constructive character. It is important for black scholars to begin their own reflection and writing on the meaning of sexuality, especially as it relates to spirituality. I recall a black husband's violent response to a co-worker who assumed that he would enjoy bringing his wife of thirty years to a "swinging party." This black husband was highly insulted precisely because he could not separate sex from the total relationship he enjoyed with his wife. For the black husband, sexuality was contextualized in a whole relationship. This goes back to our African ancestry as well as a holistic understanding of biblical faith.

If creation is good and if one has a sacramental view of human life and female/male relations, then sexuality and spirituality come together. This view exalts the sexual bond above the sordid level of objective, hedonistic perspectives. This higher level of understanding of the love bond between females and males is essential if there is to be mutual self-giving and respect between the two sexes in all of life's relationships.

It is essential that black churches begin to study sex and provide a wholesome interpretation through sex education. While black churches are aware of extensive sexual activity by many members, they have not made a bold attempt to pass on to the membership a wholesome view of sexuality between men and women. A part of the difficulty faced by black religious leaders is a lack of a comprehensive treatment of a proper view of sex. Sexuality needs to be understood against the background of an appropriate relation between men and women, generally. It also has much to do with a wholesome relation between men and women in ministry.

Black Women and Theology

Black women have a peculiar role as mediators in the face of the network of oppressions that give rise to the theologies of liberation. Oppression in multiple expressions is a part of the black woman's experience—whether of race, class, or gender. In addition, she can bring non-Western perspectives and experiences to the dialogue. In all settings, the black woman should insist that her concerns be heard and dealt with. Blackness, femaleness, and poverty are often entwined in the black woman's experience. Black women need a critical distance from white feminist theologians and black male theologians for their constructive task. Their problem and audience give them a distinctive and creative theological-ethical task.

Black women's experience of oppression is not far removed from that of black men. Their affections are associated intimately with black males as fathers, sons, husbands, friends, and lovers. There is no suggestion here that because racism has had a devastating effect upon blacks, black women should not attack sexism fostered by black men. The society has dealt and continues to deal deadly blows to black manhood. Black women cannot afford to be indifferent to the plight of black males. However, this concern must not be at the expense of the affirmation of women's own self-worth and dignity as children of God. Thus black men as well as women are invited to look realistically at the scourge of racism upon black people. Once they have sorted things out, they should seek ways to cooperate in overcoming this common foe for the sake of family, community, churches, and, of course, future generations of black people.

There may also be collaboration with white women on the common experience of oppression at the hands of men—both black and white. For example, sexual harassment is not a white-only phenomenon. Sexual abuse, subordination, and seduction of women for selfish ends know no racial distinction. This is one instance where the oppressed becomes the oppressor. Thus, many of white women's experiences of sex oppression ring true with black women in their relation with black men. Feminist theology, which is produced mainly by white and middle-class women, has a vital message for black women in society and church.

The feminization of poverty is a complicated phenomenon in the black community. Black women often head single-parent households. This means that they bear an undue burden as they care for the young. It is shameful that black men aid in conceiving children for whom they show no love or fiscal responsibility. Here again, economic factors come into play, for instance, unemployment. Black men and women need to give special attention to the well-being of black males at an early age. Such things as their education, value clarification, discipline, and preparation for employment and responsible parenthood need emphatic attention. This responsibility cannot be assumed by women alone. If it cannot be done in a two-parent family situation, it must be done in other ways. Extended families and church families can do much. Poverty and its dire consequences upon healthy black male-female relationships affect all black life.

Black womanist theology is important and timely. The issues of importance to black women go beyond those of white women or black men. Black women theologians have carved out a project of their own. It is inspired by black nationalism and black liberation theology. The term "womanist" is derived from Alice Walker's view that black women need to express their experience out of the language and ethos of the black community. At the same time, they need to use language that uniquely expresses their female experience as black people. It means being "grown," responsible, in charge, and serious about one's life.

A key exponent of womanist theology is Jacquelyn Grant. As a mature theologian, Grant, in her recent book *White Women's Christ and Black Women's Jesus* has given the most comprehensive statement on the subject thus far.[5] She suggests that womanist theology expresses the suffering and experiences of black women. It brings together issues of race, sex, and class. Thus, it provides the broadest and most comprehensive foundation for liberation theology so far. Womanist theology provides a telling critique of racism in feminist theology and sexism in black theology. Beyond these elements, womanist theology adds the dimension of class since black women are poor. Womanist theology is representative of a multidimensional analysis of oppression. Grant even suggests that the poor black woman is a "christic" figure in contemporary white society. This is reminiscent of the black theologian's reflection on the "Black Messiah." Womanist theologians may make a profound impact on all theologies of liberation.

Katie Cannon extends this womanist tradition into ethics as she uses the life and works of Zora Neale Hurston as a foundation for her reflection.[6] In addition, black women preachers in the womanist movement give wide and popular expression to gender concerns through the spoken word. Ella Mitchell has edited several volumes of their works.[7]

Several concerns are obvious: Will these theologians be able to find a significant response from lay women? How will they share the depths of their concern with black men—clergy and lay? How will they find common cause with black theologians? These are delicate matters. Many black women push men forward in their own lives as well as in the church due to the scarcity of responsible black men under forty in home or church. Black women are in the forefront of the attempt to strengthen black institutions. They will be reluctant to join any group, including their sisters, that seems to be against their efforts. While I support the efforts of womanist theologians, I am also aware that they face problems similar to those of black theologians in getting a hearing and affirmative response from the black church and community.

Several black womanist thinkers' views have not yet been fully articulated in print. I treasure the conversations I have had with Delores

Carpenter, Pauli Murray, Delores Williams, Toinette Eugene, Cheryl Gilkes, and Suzan D. Johnson. In biblical studies, I would mention Renita J. Weems and Clarice Martin. Janice Hale is well-known in religion and education. Melva Costen is well-known for her work in sacred music.[8] This is a short list of womanist thinkers, but they are those with whom it has been my privilege to work or to enter into meaningful dialogue. While the views expressed here are my own, conversation with them has enlightened and enriched my outlook on the role of black women in home, community, and church.

Mutuality of Black Men and Women: Overcoming Sexism in the Church

This final section is designed to make some suggestions regarding how to forge some understandings between black men and women in the church. A long-standing concern of mine has been that of building strong black families through the ministry of the church. The institution that has the most promise for bringing all black people together—men, women, and children—in community where there is mutual acceptance, is the church. If this happens in the church, it can have a wide impact elsewhere in our society.

Black theology is a good way to open the way to a discussion of sexism in the black church. Black theology is representative of the black religious experience, though by no means conclusive. Here the corrective of womanist theologians is readily acknowledged. When black women state their concerns, most black theologians are sensitive and offer their desire to be open and inclusive.

My colleague James H. Cone has expressed well these concerns in his preface to the 1986 edition of *A Black Theology of Liberation*. Cone first admits his "failure to be receptive to the problem of sexism in the black community and society as a whole." He speaks of his "failure" and "embarrassment" in the use of exclusive language in his early writings. But he goes on to say that language only "symbolizes" the problem. We must change language since language reflects reality, but the problem is much deeper than language, he suggests, since sexism dehumanizes and kills. What follows is Cone's powerful statement of repentance and challenge to black males, especially pastors and theologians.

Contrary to what many men say (especially preachers), sexism is not merely a problem for white women. Rather it is a problem of the human condition. It destroys the family and society, and makes it impossible for persons to create a society defined by God's intentions for humanity. Any black male theologian or preacher who ignores sexism as a central problem in our society and church (as important as racism, because they are interconnected), is just as guilty of distorting the gospel as is a white theologian who does the same with racism. If we black theologians do not take seriously the need to incorporate into our theology a critique of our sexist practices in the black community, then we have no right to complain when white theologians snub black theology.[9]

This is a prophetic and critical statement by the pioneer theologian of the black experience. I personally endorse this perspective. Not only systematic theologians, but also other black religious scholars have expressed similar concerns. For example, there are the black biblical scholars under the leadership of Cain Felder in *Stony the Road We Trod*.[10] Their number includes Renita Weems and Clarice Martin. What all this indicates, in spite of the remarks of some evangelicals, is that liberation theologies need not be "one-issue" theologies. If one is passionately opposing one kind of oppression, one can empathize with victims of other oppressions. Thus, I am able to report a major breakthrough in understanding between black brothers and sisters in theological reflection. The greater task is cultivating this dialogue and getting a response from black pastors and congregations. This book is written with that challenge in mind.

A promising aspect of this situation is that the leading black theologians are in fact "church theologians." Several men and women writing theological essays are ordained and active as preachers, teachers, or educators in various denominations. Most are active as ministers within large black denominations. They are not necessarily well received. They are often said to be too "academic." However, their status in the church as well as the academy means that they are not easily ignored. Many leading pastors are well-read in black theology. They have made good use of its insights in their work as pastors. Many seminary-educated black pastors have read deeply in black theology. In many cases they have not encountered black theology in a required course, but have read widely in the literature on their own. Black and womanist theologians do have the ear of a reasonable number of black church leaders. One would hope that their voices will soon receive a favorable response for the sake of the mission of the black church.

Black Women in Ministry

Against the background of black theological reflection we have asserted the unqualified right of women to practice ministry in the church of Jesus Christ. Those who fence the pulpit and ban women from it have asserted an authority that they do not have. It is God alone who calls humans, male and female, to minister in his redemptive cause.

All humans, female and male, bear the same image bestowed upon them by the Creator. They are redeemed by the same grace. In the context of divine love, no gender distinctions are valid. As victims of racist oppression, black men should be the first persons to welcome their sisters to a full exercise of ministry. We should not use the Bible and theological perspectives to oppose the full practice of the ministry in Word and sacrament. We know the bitter taste of oppression based on race. Why would we impose such a harsh yoke upon our black sisters?

It is not appropriate to offer as an excuse the futile argument that other women will not support a black woman in the role of pastor or ordained minister. It is not unusual for the oppressed to be insensitive to their lack of freedom. It is our responsibility to do a new thing—to do what we deem to be right. Within our understanding of the Christian understanding of God's purpose, we are challenged to be fulfilled and trust God to fulfill the divine purpose in and through us. Women often bring unique gifts to ministry. Let men encourage and empower them to be effective servants of the Word. Instead of standing in their way, men should welcome them as partners in ministry. Men should use whatever authority or influence is available to them to prepare the way for the successful witness of women through the agency of the Holy Spirit.

There are no Christian biblical or theological grounds that would prohibit anyone, called and commissioned by God to minister, from practicing fully the divine summons as servant and minister in the name of Jesus Christ. It is now inevitable that women of all races will act as ordained ministers of the church. It behooves male pastors to prepare the way for God's will to be done.

The role of women in the black church is crucial for its survival and effectiveness. It is clear that the status of black women will soon be upgraded by male leadership or by women themselves. The rationale for keeping women out of the pulpit or in subordinate positions will not be long accepted. Traditional and biblical arguments against women in ministry and in key leadership roles have lost their persuasive power. With the influx of a large number of well-educated, talented, and gifted black women in ministry and theology, conservative black ministers will find it impossible to oppose this onslaught. They will do well to begin aggressively preparing the way for mutuality with black women in all walks of life and especially in the church and its ministry. When black women come forth with total dedication of life and with sacrificial efforts to study and ready themselves for ministry, no one is in the position

The Prophethood of Black Believers

to decide that they are not agents of God's saving work in the church of Jesus Christ. If this movement is of God it will prevail. Black male ministers need to submit themselves to the guidance of the Spirit and join their sisters in God's redeeming mission on the earth. It is urgent that we seek the path of mutuality rather quickly.

8

The Black Church and Economics

POLITICAL AND ECONOMIC AFFAIRS ARE OF GREAT importance to black Americans. The black church as the lead institution in the black community has a real role in the course of political and economic affairs. The church among blacks cannot escape involvement in these areas since these factors figure so largely in the condition of black Americans. (We will look more specifically at political concerns in the next chapter.)

As soon as a black pastor takes over leadership of a congregation, he or she faces the onslaught of problems from the political and economic sectors. It is, therefore, best to anticipate these connections and give some prior consideration as to how to provide the proper guidance for constructive involvement of church people in both political and economic affairs.

The black church has been sensitive to social justice issues from its inception because it has been ministering to an oppressed people. Therefore, interpretation of the gospel of Jesus Christ in the black church tradition has been concerned about justice as well as love. Justice and love cannot be separated. To quote from an earlier book:

> The manner in which justice and love interpenetrate each other on the plane of concrete personal and social relationships may in some way transcend human language as well as thought. But on the level of human experience when the struggles of life must be engaged, there is abundant evidence that justice serves the purpose of love and that love exalts justice to a higher level.[1]

Just as God is lovingly just and deals with us through succor and demand, the black church both heals and participates in "the pushing and shoving of justice."

A Christian Perspective on the Economic Order

We cannot live by bread alone. Neither can we live without bread. It is, therefore, essential that all Christians should give some attention to understanding the economic order. Not only individuals but also social structures can be either "sinful" or "humane." Black people have too often been the victims of unjust economic structures. Black churches do not have the luxury of ignoring the sorry economic plight of the masses of black people.

In contrast to some Christian theologians, I do not limit my reflections to biblical texts, although I hold that the Bible is foundational to ethics. The centrality of the Bible is a Protestant principle. My view of the Bible is respectful but not literal. Biblical authority is central to my outlook as a theologian of the church. Therefore, it is important to seek biblical insight concerning economics.

There is, at the same time, the role of tradition in Christian history. In studying the social teachings of the church we must consider critically and carefully the long history of Christian thought and action in the field of economics.

In addition, there is much nontheological material that is useful in all ethical reflection. There are many resources from moral philosophy and the social sciences, among other things. Western civilization is Greco-Roman as well as Judeo-Christian. Beyond this there are many constructive insights from our American heritage to draw upon. For Christians, however, all these resources must be subject to scrutiny by the perspective of the Christian faith. For example, "Afrocentricity" no less than "black power" must be subject to careful examination.

The Greco-Roman background

Plato and Aristotle are our mentors. Their insights are helpful but not beyond criticism. We know that Plato had an elitist concept of social justice. The philosopher-king occcupied a privileged position in Plato's concept of the state. Those who possessed the most knowledge were exalted and entitled to the greatest justice. Plato allowed for different degrees of self-worth. Though Plato was serious about justice, his practical application of this virtue was flawed.

Aristotle is more penetrating than Plato. This famous pupil of Plato was more practical than his master. In the *Nicomachean Ethics*, Aristotle goes beyond Plato in separating social justice from the gods. Aristotle is open to experimentation in forging a just social order.

Both Plato and Aristotle are progenitors of our understanding of justice. As original classical thinkers, they stimulate our profoundest reflections on the meaning of a just social order. It is my understanding that they arrive at *equity*, but not *equality*. Equity involves for them unequal distribution of human value and human rights. Thus we cannot look to them for the final meaning of equality.

Biblical warrants

The Hebrew Bible insists that the poor, widows, women, strangers, and slaves have human rights (see, for example, Ex. 22:21; Lev. 19:10; Deut. 24:17). Justice is a fundamental virtue on which human society is based.

In the prophets (from the eighth to sixth centuries B.C.E.) social justice and love merge with the idea of salvation. The great prophets of Israel support a social order that manifests kinship and solidarity. Isaiah, Amos, Jeremiah, and Micah do not disavow the law. They affirm law for moral direction, but they delve deeper into the motivations for moral decision and action. They provide spiritual and salvific significance to that which otherwise could be sterile and lifeless.

The New Testament develops these insights of social justice in the Old Testament. Jesus subscribed to the highest manifestation of social justice in the law and the prophets. He stressed the motives and dispositions of the heart and emphasized the priority of love and the kingdom of God. The Sermon on the Mount (Matt. 5–7) is basic to Christian social ethics. The foundation for social justice can be discerned throughout the Bible.[2]

Justice appears to have the same meaning as "righteousness" in biblical terms. Righteousness connects the social justice concerns of the Hebrew scriptures with those of the entire Bible. In the New Testament righteousness is enriched by the meaning of love. When love as *agape* is associated with justice, it does not become cheap. It becomes more costly, because it is now associated with the meaning of the cross and the reconciliation that is to be manifest not only between God and sinful humans but also between the self and other persons.

The Christian church

Christians exist in this world where Caesar rather than Christ often reigns. For two thousand years we have had to make decisions and take actions based upon historical realities.

Protestantism was founded on the basis of *sola scriptura*. Yet the Bible does not provide a detailed blueprint of ethics. The biblical message must be contextualized and applied to concrete issues. Tradition, experience, facts, and the guidance of the Spirit, among other resources, are needed to make responsible moral decisions. We have freedom as Protestants to follow our consciences, but conscience must be well informed to effect worthy judgments and responsible action.

Thomas W. Ogletree provides a helpful guide to the use of the Bible in Christian ethics. His study uses the best scholarship in phenomenological thought, biblical criticism, and hermeneutics. It is not easy reading but it is worth the effort of serious reflection. He presents the foundations for this study in the first two chapters. Thereafter he works his way through the biblical texts. He shows how we can bring the biblical "horizon" together with the contemporary issues to be decided. Through the process of historical contextualization in our present, the biblical message can be a powerful guide to our decisions and actions in the moral sphere. No one provides all the answers, but Ogletree's efforts are noteworthy.[3] As Protestants who rely on biblical authority, we must put forth a serious effort to translate the Bible in the direction for responsible moral decisions.

Again, the tradition of the churches through the ages implies some knowledge of the intersection of moral philosophy with Christian theology. How has the Christian faith been influenced by ideas from outside? For example, Stoicism exerted significant influence upon Christian thought and action. In the modern and contemporary periods the external influences have speeded up their impact upon the life, thought, and actions of Christians. The progress of natural and social sciences, together with rapid changes wrought by these factors, have taxed the churches greatly to keep up and to provide guidance for the devout who must live and act under these pressures.

In our own time one may view the AIDS epidemic as a prime example of the new challenge before Christians. Here "feelings about disease and disfigurement, sex and death, futility and friendship are present without sentimentalization or false romanticism."[4] Thus in our time as in all others, the ethical concerns of the Christian faith are tested in the crucible of life-and-death decisions. Making decisions is nothing new for Christians. We need, therefore, to study the Christian tradition in applied ethics, learn from the past, and prepare for the present and future. We live in a real world of empirical realities, where decisions and actions are demanded of us.

African Roots and African American Fruits

Since 1966, black power and black consciousness have influenced black Christians. This movement has been embellished by a quest for *roots* in the African ancestral past of black Americans. This appreciation of heritage has given pride of selfhood and peoplehood to African Americans. This process has not abated. It has recently taken the form of "Afrocentricity," which is a broad-based movement especially manifest in urban school systems around the nation. There is an insistence that the worth of black people is not determined by various forms of oppression they have endured and continue to experience in this country. Afrocentricity focuses upon a noble ancestry in Africa.

This outlook has much to do with the subject matter of this chapter, the political economy. We need to look into our heritage to find clues that will assist in our economic development and our political advancement. We have often been both penniless and powerless. We need to search for appropriate means to improve our lot in American society for the sake of our generations to come.

Cornel West, among recent black religious scholars, has focused on the political economy in several books and essays. He recounts how some black religious leaders have recommended some aspects of socialism to provide the means for empowerment, both economic and political. Representatives of this outlook were George Washington Woodbey and his disciple, G. W. Slater, Jr., at the beginning of the twentieth century. West himself has often spoken of progressive Marxism and "an Afro-American revolutionary Christianity."[5]

Behind these twentieth-century efforts to make economic and political advances, I would like to point to the African emphasis upon communalism. This sense of community, rooted in a broad-based sense of kinship, is worth our examination. If it can be reclaimed, it may not only restore our sense of togetherness and mutual caring but also be a means to economic and political progress by blacks.[6] Much has been written about the African maxim, "because I am, we are!" Also the concept of *ujamaa*, "familyhood," has been used to express the basis for our African way to socialism. From the African perspective, the way to economic and political development is not the type of individualism that African Americans so readily endorse in our society.

Furthermore, in our Afro-American past we have lived by some aspects of the African perspective on economics and politics. C. Eric Lincoln describes this outlook as a dialectic between survival and liberation. If we apply this to economics, we see that, on one hand, we have often banded together to survive by sharing goods and services with one another. On the other hand, we have challenged the system to be more humane in regard to matters such as job openings, promotions, and employment opportunities.[7] Lincoln writes:

The survival strategy . . . meant to eke out a living by whatever means possible. . . . Studies of extremely poor black people have shown that

The Prophethood of Black Believers

many of them relied upon an economy of bartering, exchanging and changing goods and possessions. They also tended to rely upon an extended kinship network, of real and fictive kin.[8]

Lincoln explains that kin relations often provided the only safety net poor black people knew. This support involved such things as borrowing and lending money, moving in with kinfolk during times of severe economic hardships, sending children to live with kin while parents worked (sometimes away from home), and other radical adjustments in family structure in order to survive.

Lincoln describes this "liberation strategy":

There was a real understanding that real freedom only comes with the attainment of a measure of economic base. . . . Upward mobility . . . was important because it allowed for the possibility of devising strategies for a greater economic independence. . . . The liberation view also emphasized self-determination, dignity, and a pride in the African and African American heritage and institutions. This liberation perspective tended to be critical of those economic aspects of the capitalist system that tend to dehumanize and oppress people.[9]

Lincoln's description of the black perspective on economics is consistent with my own experience and observation. There is this tension in black life caused by the persistent oppression based upon racism. He has correctly designated it as the survival-liberation dialectic. This insight helps us to understand the black perspective on main issues, including economic and political issues, decisions, actions.

Lincoln's further observations on the roles of the black church in economic and political matters are instructive. On the one hand, the black church helps its members survive. Its economic ethic was initiated in slave quarters, where survival strategies and self-help developed out of necessity. It was essential that slaves help one another to endure the traumas and terrors of the plantation system. During illness, injury, and death, slaves assisted one another. For example, when parents died or were sold, the children were often cared for by other slaves, irrespective of kinship or lack of it. Thus this survival and self-help tradition was later to be Christianized.[10] The black church came out of this development of mutual aid or beneficial societies. The African Methodist Episcopal Church is a prime example.

On the other hand, black churches have become a means to economic liberation. Black churches urged their members to pool their meager resources to build church buildings. This was just the beginning of the black church's project of economic liberation. During Reconstruction, black congregations often took over plantations and established communities of economic uplift led by black pastors. Fraternal lodges, burial associations, black owned banks and life insurance companies, and other economic institutions sprang from black churches under ministerial or lay leadership.[11]

In the course of time the black churches became more aggressive and attacked structural forms of economic exploitation and oppression. We could refer to the founding of the Urban League in 1911, the activity of Adam Clayton Powell, Jr., who led street demonstrations on economic issues, and the work of A. Philip Randolph, who organized the Brotherhood of Sleeping Car Porters.[12]

All this church activity in the economic field led W. E. B. Du Bois to write:

> Consequently all movements for social betterment are apt to center in the churches. Beneficial societies in endless number are formed here . . . , cooperative and building associations have lately sprung up; the minister often acts as an employment agent, considerable charitable and relief work is done and special meetings held to aid special projects. The race problem in all its phases is continually being discussed, and, indeed from this forum many a youth goes forth inspired to work.[13]

What this all means is that the black church has had a constructive role in economic uplift of black people throughout its history. This continues to be the case. If the churches default on this legacy, it may mean their rapid decline. The black church must continue to seek both survival and liberation for black people in all areas of life.

Market Command Economic Systems

In many ways, capitalism and socialism are direct opposites. The free-market economy of capitalism presupposes minimal state activity. The command type of economy of socialism involves state planning of resources used, of allocation of labor, and of investments and consumption.

In this concern we are dealing with politics as well as economics. Capitalism seems to be more compatible with a climate of abundant political freedom. Socialism seems to thrive best where there is more state control. Both systems need to be carefully monitored. There are strengths and weakness in each camp.[14] In fact, we would be hard-pressed to find an economic order that is not in some manner a "mixed" economy.

We have seen radical changes take place recently in the former Soviet Union. Not even experts know exactly what the future holds. We do know, however, that for about seventy years, Marxism had a shattering impact upon the global political economy. This large influence for such a long period indicates that inherent in this form of thought and action was some truth. We need to know what that truth is. In my view the Marxist critique of capitalism needs to be taken seriously. It would be a mistake of gigantic proportions to dismiss communism (as it was manifest in the Union of Soviet Socialist Republics and Eastern Europe) and embrace fondly an individualistic and greedy form of capitalism. There is the even greater danger of identifying capitalism with a Christian manifestation of an economic order. Any acceptable Christian perspective on the economy must include both the possibility of self-fulfillment and a sharing and caring sense of community.

What we need to be most concerned about is to what extent any economic order meets human needs. Capitalism may be too tied to selfishness and greed to be acceptable to Christians. Socialism may be so caught up in collective concerns as to overlook the dignity and worth of individuals. Marxism often embraced godlessness and brutality, destroying human beings in the name of humanity. Yet there is an acceptable "communalism" inherent in the Christian ethic that is authentically human. In this regard, I earlier observed:

> An economic order which approximates the Christian ideal would need to take seriously personal rights and needs. It would need to be concerned about food, clothing, shelter, and education for each person. . . . But, at the same time, there should be sufficient government control to uphold the rights of all citizens to ensure that they as persons and families share in the prosperity of the nation. From a Christian point of view social justice should never be traded off for prosperity. . . . The economic order should enhance persons-in-community as humans work together with God for the realization of the Beloved Community.[15]

Economic Outlook for Blacks

Here we are concerned with the present economic situation for blacks. Much of the annual Urban League report on "Black America" deals with the economic factor.[16] This is a definitive report. What we discuss here will be more in the nature of an overview.

There was a time when only a few professional opportunities were open to blacks. These required considerable formal education, except for the pastorate. Even so, a goodly number of ministers went to college and seminary. Sometimes the minister was among the best-educated people in a small community. Many teachers with college degrees ran the local segregated schools. There were a few doctors, dentists, morticians, and other people in helping professions. In addition, there were skilled laborers, service personnel, and the like. Most of these people served their own people. In some cases they served the larger interracial community as well. The vast majority of black folk were hired servants in the majority community, working for minimum wages, if they had employment at all. I grew up in such an environment in the South.

Education was viewed as the way out of this dependent economic situation. For example, black teachers lived well according to the economic standards in small communities. Black teachers were also role models and counselors to black youth. They were highly regarded by black parents. Often they were active in black churches. Many taught Sunday school and served as lay leaders.

Many black men were self-taught carpenters, bricklayers, and plasterers. Some graduated to the level of contractors and passed their skills on to their sons. In some cases these skilled laborers sent their sons to trade schools or technical colleges. However, daughters were usually given priority for higher education. Because of the potential for exploitation of black females by white men, parents did not want their daughters to be maids. This created an imbalance between black men and women that has never been corrected insofar as education and culture are concerned.

The migration into the urban ghettos upset this steady uplift of blacks through higher education. Patterns of family life as well as economic patterns of progress have been aborted.[17] What we face now are broken homes, extreme cases of unemployment, underemployment, homelessness, and an epidemic of AIDS and drugs. A mass of hopeless black folk are outside the American social system. A large and growing underclass is developing as an American tragedy. Although they are mainly "out of sight and out of mind," this large black underclass is a major threat to the stability of this society. It is a real time bomb. The need to address this problem also has an economic dimension. The United States cannot maintain its lead in the "new world order" with the waste of so much human potential.

Our middle class has changed its focus. In the past, the black middle class served other blacks. The "haves" helped the "have-nots." Today's black middle class is more individualistic. Some blacks who have been educated in Ivy League institutions have turned their intellect against winning freedom for other blacks. They have joined the chorus of those who say that blacks do not deserve further assistance to win their equality after almost four hundred years of racist oppression. They charge their own, still struggling for justice, with discrimination in reverse when

The Prophethood of Black Believers

black Americans ask the society to be fair. They have become avowedly individualistic in outlook. These people have forgotten from whence they came. They have abandoned the black underclass.

A materialistic secularity has become a driving force for many middle-class blacks. During the last decade or so the driving force for acquiring higher education has been economic security. I often hear parents talk in glowing terms about sons and daughters preparing to make a lot of money. One seldom hears the same praise for those who plan to give their lives to the education of the young. The praise now goes to those who will be corporate lawyers and business tycoons. Even medicine, as a profession, is now pushed into the background. There is more money to be made elsewhere. This individualism fed by materialistic secularism or pure greed is antithetical to the personal and communal uplift of black people.

Even many educational programs in black colleges are geared to instant financial success. In the past, black colleges provided moral and religious education together with a sound liberal arts education for everyone. It is now possible to bypass the fine arts and humanities and go immediately into computer science, the natural sciences, and business administration. The humanities, fine arts, great literature, and the like are being neglected in order to prepare for making big money. For these and other reasons, it is not hard to explain why the black community is split apart ideologically and economically. The Clarence Thomas syndrome is devastating to the uplift of black people, but it is very present and must be engaged decisively and urgently.[18] Blacks who are trying to make it in the corporate world are obsessed by the American dream of prosperity.[19] Here we refer to the tendency of some upwardly mobile blacks to seek their own success while distancing themselves from the plight of the majority of black people.

There is also the fact that blacks are mainly consumers rather than entrepreneurs. This means that they are easily exploited. The most bizarre forms of consumerism are manifest among black youth in poverty. The desire for designer jackets, expensive gold trinkets, and athletic shoes has led many of our young people into the drug trade. This only reflects the consumerism of the larger society, including some parents, who overvalue material things.

In 1978, a black businessman, D. Parke Gibson, wrote a disturbing book, *$70 Billion in the Black*,[20] an account of the habits of America's black consumers. Gibson's book indicates that blacks spend money on goods that many want and do not need. This obsession with having expensive "things" for their own sake sabotages racial uplift. One's life does not consist of what one possesses. Character is far more important. As we teach values to the young, this point must be driven home.

There is some concern among public school educators regarding what is called value-education. This movement is growing nationwide, especially in large urban areas where crime among children is soaring. Educators realize that they have children in their care for a significant amount of time and that they must be role models, surrogate parents, and providers of moral guidance for youth who have no other institutional support. In Philadelphia and Washington, D.C., for example, such education projects are taking shape. In Philadelphia thirteen schools are developing a "cluster" to instill values in children. For example, public schools and one Roman Catholic school are coordinating these efforts. This pilot project has the support of School Superintendent Constance Clayton. Thus, all the feeder schools are working across the thirteen-year span with each student to instill values. In a similar effort in Washington, the program is citywide, involving more than eighty thousand students.

It is essential that the value programs relate to economic factors. Children need to be taught the relative value of material possessions. They need to know what it is to establish worthy goals for a meaningful life. They need to know that life is God-given and precious. Altruism and service to others are essential for a workable social order. Most of all, teachers in value education must not partake of the Elijah syndrome ("I alone am left," 1 Kings 19:10). They must realize that there are others who care, especially parents and churches. A way must be found to get various groups together for mutual support in this important effort.

The Challenge of the Economic Ministry of Black Churches

Concern for the economic condition of black people is generally a present reality for both pastor and people. The decline of economic resources impacts the offering receipts. The minister's family income and the support for vital programs are affected by any economic distress. When, for example, Mayor Sharon Pratt Kelly threatened to cut out hundreds of middle-management jobs in Washington, D.C., several black pastors publicly opposed this action as unjustified and inhumane.

The economic challenges to black churches are so numerous that they may only be touched on here. Pastors and congregations will need to choose their own projects for action after deciding the greatest economic needs in their locale. Also, larger efforts—city-wide, state-wide—would be needed in order to effect changes that move beyond pacification to liberation for black people in the economic sphere. Black churches should support sanctions against businesses that earn large sums of money from black people but practice racial discrimination in various ways.

Gender problems, insofar as economics are involved, are family problems. When we speak of the "feminization of poverty," we may have in mind only the plight of black women themselves. It is fitting that we should stress the problems peculiar to black women in order to place in clear relief the magnitude of black women's economic distress. Even so, we must see black women's economic condition in the context of a racist society. Most blacks are poor. We must immediately give similar attention to black men and children—in fact, to the entire family.

This is especially true in view of the desire of most black women to have children and to attempt to establish stable family life with a father and with offspring. Womanist theologians have helped us to understand the aspirations of black women. Next, let us hope womanists will turn their attention to black family life. Their input is greatly needed for balance.

Black women in the mass have several critical economic concerns. They receive low wages. They are oppressed as blacks, as women, and as those in poverty. It has been documented that women (all women) with college degrees earn salaries equal to men with high school degrees. Many of these black women have children; this accounts for such a large number of black children in poverty.

Race enters this discussion, for black men are also oppressed and do not have, even with college degrees, the earning power of white males. Statistical reports often speak of women as if all women are treated the same. In a racist society it is unfair to lump statistics on minority women with those on women in general. We must separate the status of white women from nonwhite women. White women are related to the power brokers of American society. Their protest will be heard first since they at least move in some of the same spheres as the power brokers. They will enter the boardrooms while other women are still oppressed. Whatever women have in common must be carefully and critically assessed. For instance, a two-parent, two-salary white household is often compared with a black female-headed household with several children. Even when the black husband is present, the combined income of husband and wife is often similar to that of a white male alone.

Ideally, husbands would be present in black households, and that would be a welcome relief. The usual situation, due to prison incarceration of so many black males, is quite different. There is an intolerable incidence of unemployment of black males. Underemployment is also common. Even if employed, the black male is usually subordinate to the white male in authority and income. The victimized black woman is close to the black man who is also victimized by our economic system. The black male is son, father, husband to the black woman. Racism victimizes all those who are near and dear in the black family, church, and community. Many are caught up in a web of oppression from which they have not been able to escape.

Housing patterns are also determined by both economics and race. Race is as powerful as economics in determining where one must live. Economic means is not always the deciding factor. White neighbors may not want blacks nearby, and real estate brokers often steer clients to neighborhoods where they think they belong. An experiment in housing in Chicago illustrates how the living environment transforms values for the young. Black inner-city families were moved into the suburbs, where jobs were more abundant and accessible. Schools were better and parents observed that their children were safer. The result was a remarkable improvement in the attitudes and values of the children in the black families involved. Since there is an economic factor here that determines environment, here is a clear challenge for black churches. Better housing for blacks, even in the middle class, is hampered by white racism in economic institutions. Bank loans for mortgages are often not accessible even to two-income black families. Black churches should be selective in banking. Their funds should not be deposited in banks that practice any form of discrimination based upon race, class, or gender.

Although much more could be written about the economic factors in the black experience, this chapter provides sufficient theological, ethical, racial, and economic reflection to set before us the challenge for ministry in the economic sphere. I close by repeating what I observed in the beginning: We cannot live by bread alone, but neither can we exist without bread.

The Prophethood of Black Believers

9

The Black Church and Politics

THIS CHAPTER IS ABOUT MINISTRY IN BLACK churches in light of political realities. Those who minister to an oppressed and suffering community must face political realities. After all is said and done, those at the bottom of the social order face survival issues. "Self-help" has recently been bandied as a cure-all for the needs of the black underclass. Self-help has a long and effective history among black people. The significant progress blacks have made in many areas of life is a concrete testimony to the self-help tradition. This tradition should be maintained. However, in light of the oppression and repression of racism, there is a need for massive and continuous government assistance to right the wrongs visited upon black people for hundreds of years in this society.

Blacks have been in this country since 1619. For more than two hundred years they provided free labor for the building of the economy of this nation. Blacks helped to build railroads and fought in all the wars. In fact, in every way possible blacks have earned their place as full and authentic citizens of the United States. We are now more than a century and a quarter beyond chattel slavery and yet blacks are still struggling to win rights that are routinely given to citizens recently arrived from other parts of the globe. Racism is for black Americans an intergenerational problem that will not go away.

Full opportunity for political participation is a recent privilege. Blacks have been free to labor, first as slaves and subsequently at survival wages, when work has been available. Middle-class blacks have been able to lift themselves to some measure of comfort. This achievement has been mainly through great determination, hard work, and taking full advantage of affirmative-action initiatives. The black underclass has, at the same time, slid lower and lower into the quagmire of misery. There is a need now for political enlightenment of the mass black population, who seem not to appreciate or understand fully the importance of the ballot for their own uplift. This need suggests a significant role for ministers and churches in the political sphere. We turn now to some theological and ethical reflections on the political realities that Christians must face.

The Church-State Relation

In origin the state appears to be both artificial and natural. There must have been more or less conscious and deliberate purpose in its formation. Yet behind the state-forming activity there were involuntary social and political needs that sought satisfaction. These latter needs have their roots in human nature. Aristotle stated this fact when he referred to humans as "political animals." The state-forming dispositions in humans are deeper than conscious volition. Thus, it may be said that the state has its ultimate foundation in human nature rather than in the human will. In this sense the state may be regarded as resulting from natural growth, and from the religious point of view it may be seen as an order of divine creation.[1]

The psychological needs that enter into the foundation and structure of the state are numerous. One of these is the need for fellowship or community. This need is innate and is rooted in God's creative purpose. Humans are by disposition gregarious. Sociability is inherent in them. We are born to live together, and apart from this sense of community we are not truly human. The state is the broadest expression of full community life, apart from humanity itself, and in this respect it is necessary to a complete satisfaction of human sociability.

There is also the psychological need for the realization of justice. Without justice there can be no security, peace, or cooperation. Justice is difficult to define, but humans know in a profound inner sense when they are being treated unjustly. Justice is a human right. It is etched upon the human psyche. To establish justice, therefore, is of primary importance to human life, and to do so is the distinctive function of the state.

Over against a totally pessimistic concept of the state, in which justice is subordinated to power, is a more ethical perspective. It asserts that the state has its chief roots in its citizens' need for justice, a need that could be met only by the state's possession of awesome power. However, power does not come first, but second. It was not power that created right but right that created power. In other words, the power of the state is instrumental rather than intrinsic. The state has its source in its people's need for a just and secure social order, an order that can be realized only through the exercise of adequate power. The unethical use of power is not inherent in the nature of the state. Good and evil are as mixed in the state as in the individual. The ethics of the state differ in some respects from those of the individual, but there is no reason to ascribe only demonic possession to the state.

The state is the collective will, and as such there is no reason why it, as well as the individual, should not be capable of being moralized. Apart from individuals, the state is an abstraction. It follows that the individual alone is concrete and that moral principles of the state reflect those held by individuals in the state unless the state be totalitarian and there is no voice from the *demos*. Even then the moral principles of the state will be those of the individuals in power. Thus the state should be viewed as a moral agent.[2]

This analysis, however, can be complicated by racism. This historically has been the case in the United States, where blacks are a minority. However, racism has been manifest in South Africa where blacks are the majority but until recently have been voteless. Nazism is an example of a regime in which the obsession with power was reinforced by anti-Semitism, a form of racism. Thus theologians like Martin Luther King Jr., Alan Boesak, and Dietrich Bonhoeffer have a special message to illustrate these abuses of state power where racism is a powerful factor in the political sector.

The use of power determines its moral content, as Martin Luther King Jr. argues in *Where Do We Go from Here: Chaos or Community?*[3] Power may be used for good or evil ends. Sovereignty does not imply absolute and unlimited power. It refers to adequate power to accomplish the proper goals of the state. It involves the rule of reason and conscience. It recognizes the normal interests and rights of humans and the duty of the state to protect these rights and interests. Instead of seeking to suppress or absorb them, the true state will encourage their development insofar as they minister to the spiritual and physical welfare of the people. The state's own supreme authority will cooperate with the lesser authorities present in every normal and progressive human society. The state, then, is to provide a context within which human beings shall have room to lead the good life.

A provisional conclusion regarding proper church-state relations implies a complementary relation. The state is to uphold justice and protect human rights. It is to restrain hindrances to the good life citizens have in common. The church affirms loyalty to a higher standard and source of value, the kingdom of God. Its source of life and action is the ethic of love. It therefore stands in judgment upon all human situations, whether individual or collective, including its own life. It is only when the church is self-critical that it brings the proper credentials to political thought and action.

Christian Faith and Political Realism

Black people have constantly sought a place to stand in reference to political realities in the United States. Politics for black Americans have been filled with ambiguities and dilemmas. Eric Lincoln has referred to this perplexed situation as a dialectic of survival-liberation.[4] James H. Cone, in a recent book, describes the situation as a "dream" or "nightmare" as viewed by Martin Luther King Jr. or Malcolm X.[5] This conflict in the experience of black people renders the political situation most difficult to understand. Because of the great injustices spawned by racism, black Americans find it difficult to know how to participate constructively in the political process. The role of government is not immediately apparent. The *how* and *why* of participation in politics is often confused. Our first consideration against this background should be to outline some political realities. Wherever we come out ideologically, there needs to be a goal of constructive use of political power for liberation above and beyond mere survival.

Donald E. Messer in *Christian Ethics and Political Action* has stated extremely well what we should mean by "political realities" in this hard-hitting volume that every minister involved in political action should read. He begins by insisting that politics is an "obligation" rather than an "option" for Christians. What he is saying is that as citizens we are inevitably involved, even when we are inactive. If upright people with high ethical ideals withdraw from the political arena, the most unethical and ambitious people will dominate the political sector. Because politics has an impact upon one's entire life and the society in which one lives, there is no neutral zone for Christians. Those who see politics as too "dirty" to get involved in are not facing the real world, Messer insists.[6] Like Waldo Beach, he would recommend that those who get involved should bring the "facts" and their "faith-premises" together. In this way Christians can have a constructive influence upon the course of political action. Beach writes: "The question then becomes, not whether religion and politics should mix, but what form the inevitable mix should take."[7]

A very sensitive area for church involvement is "partisan" politics. We are reminded that Christians should be involved as individuals but also as members of corporate bodies. We are also part of a pluralistic society with many ideologies and religions. We need to be aware of the possibility of coalitions with believers who think differently and nonbelievers who share some of our ethical goals. We must not stake all on "one-issue" goals at the expense of wider humanitarian interests. Again, what we may be able to support as individuals may be antithetical to the goals of the majority of persons in our congregation or in our denomination.[8]

A personal experience with an issue like abortion could lead one to be passionately for or against it.

Because of the religious freedom we enjoy in this country, the church can be "the conscience of the nation." Churches are free to speak and work for changes that they see as desirable in the social and political life of the nation. Churches can pass resolutions, lobby, mount protest demonstrations, and publicize their views on central issues facing the country.

Black denominations illustrated this freedom of religious expression well during the summer of 1991 as they opposed the Clarence Thomas nomination to the Supreme Court. The Progressive Baptist Convention, under the leadership of Pastor Charles Adams, made an all-out effort to stop the nomination. The resolution before this body was well prepared and presented. It was supported by top leaders in this body. Dr. Gardner Taylor made the final appeal that swayed majority opinion. The Progressives joined forces with the National Baptist Convention, which happened to be meeting in Washington at this momentous time. Dr. Adams was asked to speak on behalf of most black Baptists on Capitol Hill in opposition to the Thomas nomination. This statement was said to be supported by between twelve and fifteen million black Baptists nationwide. Even though this effort appeared to be futile given the political trends in Washington, it was worthwhile. It gave black people in these denominations a practical lesson in political thought and action. Those involved began to realize the necessity of church action in the political field. They noted how well the action was carried out and that together, through powerful religious assemblies, blacks can claim the right to be heard. One would hope that this type of political involvement could be translated into votes. For example, we need several black senators on Capitol Hill.

The church can be a "servant-critic" of the state. We should never equate patriotism and Christianity. While politicians have always courted servanthood of religious bodies toward the state, they have often been offended when churches and/or church leaders have criticized the state. The function of critic is very difficult for the church to perform for several reasons. First, as we have seen, the critic function is rejected by many politicians. Messer writes: "The powerful of this earth do not usually take kindly to the suggestion that their work or politics are not in harmony with God."[9]

Second, the critic role requires courage and conviction. For those who, in their attraction to the Christian community, want to withdraw from the world, there is no zeal for politics. If Christians believe that faith and politics do not mix and that personal faith is unrelated to major ethical and political questions in the society, they see politics as off-limits to their faith.

Third, Christian answers to political questions are hard to generate. Christians who deal in absolutes often do not grapple with the harsh realities and dilemmas of life and thus fail to recognize there is room for disagreement among devout and conscientious Christians. It is also hard to forge a consensus in the face of complex facts and awesome challenges in the world of politics.

Black churches need to examine the danger of corporate church involvement as well as the privilege and impact of such involvement. There is always the possibility that the gospel may be reduced to an ideology. There is also the possibility that ministers may get "bought" and "sold" on a political auction block. In 1991 in Washington, D.C., it became evident that some outstanding black pastors had gotten too close to Mayor Marion Barry. Many had the mayor's support for significant uplift projects. As the mayor's personal life began to cave in, these ministers found it difficult to be responsible critics of the District of Columbia government and its leadership. Whereas a ministers' group known as "the committee of 100" had been a political force to reckon with during the tenure of Mayors Walter Washington and Marion Barry, Mayor Sharon Pratt Kelly glided into office without their full support. Mayor Kelly (formerly Dixon) had a very rocky relationship with church leaders at first. Their loss of influence was so great, in association with Barry, that their support seemed irrelevant to the new mayor. Fortunately, a more congenial association began to develop as the new mayor sought to implement her programs throughout the District of Columbia. This case illustrates, however, the danger of churches and pastors becoming only a servant to politicians. There is always a need to be a constructive critic.

A word needs to be said about basing one's political judgments on an infallible Bible or finding direct answers in the teachings of Jesus for tough political issues. Serious and critical biblical study is needed to discern the message of the Bible for specific political decisions and actions. Jesus did not give policy directives. He spoke in generalities about values, repentance, feeding the hungry, and promoting peace and reconciliation. Jesus stressed the nature of God as self-giving love. He called his followers to respond by loving God, neighbor, and self. He summoned others to a loving life, but he did not prescribe in detail how one should respond to great policy questions. He did, however, provide clues as to what actions are more loving and gave us the motivation to act accordingly.

As a result, Christians through the centuries have understood the "social teachings of the churches" in diverse ways. Ernst Troeltsch, in *Social Teachings of the Christian Churches*, has treated this dilemma in classic form. According to Troeltsch, those who accept the impossibility of perfect love in the world and take responsibility for helping to govern political life with its ambiguities and compromises are "the church type." The "sect type" Christians withdraw from the world of politics in order to seek to maintain moral perfection. John Howard Yoder, a contemporary pacifist theologian, may represent a third type. Yoder insists that Jesus taught that we should leave things to God instead of trying to give human direction to history. Jesus did not attempt to manage history; rather, he challenged its assumptions. The Christian witnesses to the good and the most loving course, regardless of political consequences.

Black Christians have not yet fully thought through a theological rationale for mixing faith and politics. If one seeks a logical explanation that moves smoothly from faith to politics, one is not likely to find it. Often black Christians hold to the same theological views as whites in their denomination and yet are more socially concerned and politically active in applying their faith toward social transformation. It has been the main challenge of black theology to undergird this political activism with a theological foundation.

Black Church Theology and Political Involvement

First we must define what is meant by "Black Church Theology." This designation indicates here the necessary relation between the doing of theology and the mission and ministry of the black church. It would be unfortunate for theology to lapse into ideology. This does not mean that one engaged in theological reflection should not be informed by ideas and perspectives available in the thought-life of black people. It rather means that the theologian, with a set of Christian theological convictions, interprets all such ideas and perspectives from faith-premises rooted in an affirmation of faith.

For example, black history is peopled with men and women whose ideas have had a powerful effect upon the outlook of black Americans. Persons like W. E. B. Du Bois, Sojourner Truth, Booker T. Washington, and Margaret Walker are representative. During more than two hundred years of black church history they have produced the formal expression of ideas that have been the basis for a theology of protest against social injustices. A serious engagement with black theological discourse will incorporate insights from this rich political tradition. Often the model employed has been reflection and action, action and reflection.[10] In his powerful volume *Martin and Malcolm and America*, James H. Cone has insisted that "integrationism" and "nationalism" represent the two broad streams of black political thought in response to slavery and discrimination in America.[11] Eric Lincoln speaks of the dialectic of "survival" and "liberation." These are ways of speaking broadly of options that are available to black Americans as they seek to bring about constructive change in social conditions.[12]

Jesse Jackson represents both the black church and politics well. Jesse, according to the political scientist Roger D. Hatch, is one who links non-electoral forms of political mobilization and protest with traditional electoral politics.[13] James M. Washington seems to sum up the outlook of Jesse Jackson well as he writes about the "symbolic politics of black Christendom." Washington concludes that Jesse is more than a creature of the mass media. His roots are deeply planted within the black church's tradition of social, political, and economic activism.[14]

As we gather up the ideological threads and apply these to political action, it is important to remind ourselves that the black perspective is "holistic." Even our way of thinking is "both-and." It is a misnomer to juxtapose "self-help" to programs of uplift. We see clearly that we should teach our children to be industrious. At the same time we must struggle to remove obstructions to their freedom. Government programs to help the oppressed should be evaluated apart from the effort and ability of people to improve their own life situation. The involvement of black churches in the political arena illustrates a comprehensive approach to survival and liberation.

Before making a final statement on black theology and the black church's ministry, I will briefly reflect upon three areas of political concern—electoral politics, criminal justice, and waste disposal. In these and other areas of political thought and action, black ministers and theologians may understand and act politically with a particular angle of vision. In fact, blacks will view these matters for thought and action "from the bottom up."[15]

The black church has always been "political." However, in the black church politics tends to center on powerful personalities. This is a different climate from a political outlook that focuses on "issues." Blacks are often less effective as they move from church politics to electoral politics, from personalities to issues.

Black voting in urban areas where there is a large black population has resulted in many black mayors, in the South as well as in the North. Blacks have had less success in races for governor and state assemblies than in the national Congress (House of Representatives). It is a disgrace that we have had little success in the U.S. Senate, to say nothing of the White House. The only black senator in recent years was Senator Brooke of Massachusetts, who is no longer present in the Senate. Senator Braun of Illinois is now our sole black senator. One of the mistakes Jesse Jackson may have made is to seek the presidency rather than a seat in the Senate (say, from South Carolina). From the perch of an authentic Senate seat his transition to the White House could have been a distinct possibility.

The Prophethood of Black Believers

What we need to consider in the future are the facts of the real world of politics. We need to know more about the political process, the relation between money and power, the nature of networking, the issues to be addressed and how. More effort must be put forth to get people out to vote, and yet effectiveness in politics will require much more. It is not adequate merely to mix religion and politics; we must determine how they mix in order to effect changes to benefit black people. Major cities need "think tanks" where black ministers and experts in black politics exchange ideas, tactics, and strategies for political action to improve life for oppressed people. Black seminaries should offer courses of this type in the preparation of ministers. They should also provide workshops for pastors who need to be well-informed as they enter this world of *real politics*. Howard University Divinity School has an ideal location for taking the lead.

Centers like the Joint Center for Political Studies in Washington have not thus far invited religious scholars into their ranks, to my knowledge. One of the lacks in such efforts is the failure to invite minister-scholars, who are anchored in both church and academy, to participate in studies for the uplift of black people. The black church remains the one institution with unlimited possibilities for the humanization of black life. It comes in for its share of criticism for not living up to its potential. One way to realize greater effectiveness would be to provide the means to inform and prepare a new generation of church leaders, well schooled in electoral politics. Jesse Jackson and also Ronald Walters (political scientist at Howard University) and others would be outstanding resource persons for such a noble endeavor. In the future black ministers will need to have the facts, the know-how, and all the tools for decisive political involvement for the sake of their people. The black church "mixes" faith and politics; we are already deeply involved, but now we must be concerned as to how to make our Christian witness in politics more effective.

It is instructive to observe the relationship between black ministers/churches and black mayors. When I received the annual religious award from the National Conference of Black Mayors in 1983, I saw the affinity between black clergy and mayors. Many of the black mayors seemed to be devout church men and women. Some mayors, like Andrew Young, were actually ordained ministers. Most black mayors received their major political support from black churchgoers. Yet there was a sense in which the relationship was ambiguous and tense. Many blacks do not understand the political process and why the mayor has to work for the common good.

We turn now to criminal justice. As human beings we live in an imperfect world. Humans are sinful. There is also collective sin and evil. The state must have the power to restrain the individual evildoer and thwart the collective hindrances to the good life. There is the need for laws to regulate relationships between persons and communities and also between nations. These laws should be impartial and just. They should not discriminate against persons because of race, gender, or class. Sometimes social structures become "sinful." Laws are applied in an unjust manner. The police powers of the state are abused. Video cameras have recently forced society to acknowledge what black males have known all the time, that police often use brutal and excessive force in the arrest of black people, women as well as men. There is a disrespect for black life in the streets and also in the courts. Racism endemic to U.S. society explains much. Poverty is also a factor. Poor people are more often abused by law enforcers and legal practitioners than persons of wealth, especially those with white skin.

There is another factor of which black persons must be aware. Since black life is considered cheap, offenses against fellow black people are treated with leniency. Crimes of blacks against whites are prosecuted rigorously by the courts. Black ministers have often had to protest the indifferent manner in which homicide within the black community has been treated. Thus, at the same time that we have had to protest the harshness of the criminal justice system in many cases of capital punishment, we have had to protect the decent black citizen against the laxity of the criminal justice system on the home front.

Again, as we observe the large percentage of black males warehoused in our prisons, we must raise some critical questions about justice. Many social and political ramifications are associated with the prison population of blacks. I can mention only a few here. We know well the horrible conditions of the black underclass. The human jungle out of which many of our black youth come is a fertile context for breeding criminals. This potential has been reinforced by the use and abuse of drugs. Yet all black males are the victims of undue harassment by police in our urban centers. There is a sense in which the police and the courts have conspired to give every black male a criminal record. If a black male is arrested, for any cause, it is almost certain that he will spend some time behind prison bars. It is unusual for any black male to be released by a judge in the custody of even the most responsible black father. This and other reasons explain why the U.S. government spends more money to warehouse black males than for college tuition. At the same time the federal government denies a college-bound black male $5,000 for a year's tuition, $15,000 a year is spent on a black male's prison confinement.

There is something intolerable about locating city jails, and even maximum security prisons, in black neighborhoods. Some time ago I visited a penitentiary in the Baltimore slums. The young black males who grew up in that neighborhood assumed that one day they would be incarcerated. It was a part of the initiation into manhood. People on the streets would speak to prisoners they knew looking out from behind bars. Fathers, older brothers, uncles, even grandfathers in jail were "role models" for boys on the street who saw prison as their only destiny. I had to ask, how could this be? How could black ministers and churches be blind to this evil? This was such an obvious destructive force that surely black churches should rise up and use their political strength to remove this evil influence from their midst for the sake of the youth. When I see prostitutes, white and black, sitting on the steps of a black church, I am equally concerned about role models for black females. Both kinds of problems must be addressed by black churches. Not to protest such evil reveals a limited understanding of the gospel. By our indifference we provide a permissive climate for evils to grow.

We turn now to the natural environment. Black Christians have a lot to offer as we look at ecological problems. Animal rights, global warming, deforestation, oil spills, loss of species, overconsumption, and pollution of natural resources—all types of problems in the natural environment must be of concern to all Christians. God is the creator and sustainer of the total created order. The divine purpose is directed toward a positive attitude to creation that sustains life. There is, however, a special perspective or emphasis that black Christians can bring to concerns about a good natural environment. Here again there is a good reason for political thought and action.

The recent witness of Dr. Ben Chavis, who heads the Racial Justice Commission of the United Church of Christ, is exemplary. Chavis has pointed to the location of city dumps, landfills, and waste incinerators in black neighborhoods as a cause for alarm and political action. This has been the case for many years, but informed by the theology of ecology, Chavis has turned his attention to this problem that unduly affects black people. Black churches must address this problem. If black churches use their influence by acting collectively, there is no reason why this type of problem cannot be corrected at once. With his background in black theology at Howard University and at Union Theological Seminary, Chavis has well demonstrated how black theology can have a broad relevance in active ministry.

In the political arena, what black churches are able to do to bring about constructive change has much to do with their self-understanding. Thought and action stem from their interpretation of the gospel. Calvin Butts, pastor of the Abyssinian Baptist Church in Harlem, often makes a distinction between what he calls "the old time black religion" and "the new black religion." The old time black religion, he observes, was concerned with survival and preparing for the future life. The new black religion, as he defines it, is holistic. It does not give up the celebrative aspects of black religion, but it is concerned with all of life. Certainly political involvement is characteristic of the ministry of Calvin Butts, as it was for Adam Clayton Powell Jr., who preceded him. I would hasten to add that protest against injustices has coexisted with the succor and comfort needed for survival that has been there all the time. The way we blend survival and liberation in black religion is most important for political thought and action. Butts and others like him seem to find this blend in their ministry.

Summary

For black Christians, the views of the state in Romans 13 and Revelation 13 both contain some truth. Due to human sinfulness and sociability, the state has positive and negative roles. It brings constructive benefits, it delivers goods and services, it has responsibility for all citizens. But in its most negative expression, the state can become wed to the status quo. In this form it often establishes religion as a sanctifying force. The church then becomes a servant of the state and gives up its role as critic. It is a short step from the domestication of the church in the state to a demonic union of religion and statecraft. We see this diabolical expression of the state in Revelation, where the state is described as Babylon.

There is, however, a constructive role for the state. It can uphold law and order and can hinder the obstructions to the good life. The state can provide for human rights and it can be a means to insure the common good. In the United States, political bodies must face the reality of sinful social structures. There is ever present the possibility of discrimination based upon race. This is often increased by gender and class discrimination. However, these forms of oppression are different and must be remedied in diverse ways. Christians have the challenge to bring the critique of the gospel to bear upon any form of dehumanization. In some cases their faith will lead to active political protest. Some Christians may need to be politicians. There is no escape from politics in a world where good and evil are often mixed.[16]

A theological ethical foundation for political thought and action is based upon love, justice, and power.[17] The love of Christians is anchored in a God of power who is lovingly just. Love is to be expressed toward the self as well as toward the neighbor. Justice assures that love is supported by moral rectitude. Justice reaches into the public sector where law and politics hold sway. Power is an enabling force for good or evil. When we speak of the all-power of God, we refer to the ability to realize goodness in creation and through human affairs. Power is to be used to serve love and fulfill justice. With this perspective, black churches and their leaders may be a critical and redemptive force in humanizing the political order.

The Prophethood of Black Believers

10

The Music Ministry in Black Churches

THIS CHAPTER IS A THEOLOGIAN'S REFLECTIONS ON black sacred music, primarily as it is used in the worship context. It is not an interpretation by a musicologist with competence in the theory or practice of music. Jon Michael Spencer uses the term *theomusicology* to describe the kind of approach intended here. Spencer defines this term as: "musicology as a theologically informed discipline."[1]

Music is such an important resource in the life of black people that it belongs in any discussion about ministry in black churches. Music is one of the "gifts of black folk." It has a certain "soul" flavor that dramatizes the solidarity of all African people—on the African continent and in the diaspora. Music sets the atmosphere for a meaningful worship experience in black churches. Only the sermon is invested with more awe than the musical renditions in black worship. Music is at the heart of worship in the black church. It attracts youth and it has a special power to generate intergenerational fellowship. Music is, therefore, to be discussed as a force with great influence in the effective ministry to black people.

Roots of Black Music

The roots of black music, like black religion itself, were in Africa. Black people brought their aptitude for rhythmic music with them to the New World. Thus, any history of black music must begin with its African roots. The work of Ashenafi Kebede, an authority on African ethnomusicology, is helpful at this point. Kebede's *Roots of Black Music* is quite technical and comprehensive, discussing vocal expression, instruments, and dance in Africa and Afro-America. We are here focusing only on African roots in black music, with special reference to the use of music in worship. Some of Kebede's references to our area of interest follow.[2]

The origin of music in Africa is in animal sounds and is attributed to supernatural sources as well as individual composers. For example, the Ashanti link the sound of the drum to a beautiful dark bird in the forest, the *kokoyinaka*. This bird is sacred and the people claim kinship with it. It is every drummer's totem, for it is said to have taught the Ashanti how to drum. Imitation of bird calls is popular in African cultures.

In Sierra Leone, a small boy is credited with discovering *balanji* xylophone music, which is said to be an imitation of bird song. The boy, according to tradition, was about ten years of age. As he went to his father's farm early one morning, he heard a little bird whistling in the woods. The voice of the bird was melodious. The boy was so impressed that he stopped and listened to its song. Then he went on his way, cut some sticks, and shaped them flat. He cut another two sticks, arranged the first sticks on his lap, and struck the first sticks with the latter. The boy played the song he picked up from the bird. This song is said to be played by every balanji player.

Music also came into being through association with godly figures. The gods of Egypt were closely identified with music. The god Thoth was said to be an inventor of music. The dwarf Bes was lord of music and dancing. Most religious rituals were accompanied by music. Supernatural powers were attributed to music.

A more direct supernatural influence may be observed in West African communities, from whence most African Americans came. In West African communities some music was dedicated to and named after diverse deities. The Yoruba, the Dohomeans, and the Ewe of Togo and southern Ghana worship Afa, the god of divination. *Yewe* music, named after Yewe, the god of thunder and lightning, is considered one of the most highly developed forms of sacred music in African traditional history.

A few years ago I had the privilege of attending an educational conference in Togo sponsored by Leon Sullivan's OIC International. More than two hundred African Americans were a part of this cultural exchange trip. Several African Americans were middle-class retirees who had traveled widely in Europe but had never been to Africa. Upon being put in touch with their African kinfolks and the collective memory of their ancestors, they were deeply moved. Some shed tears of joy and sorrow. It was particularly in the sharing of religion and music that our spirits blended. During a devotional breakfast seminar an African brother said to me, "Now we know there is only one African people!" All the people assembled said "Amen!"

Kebede is correct, I think, in posing both a theory of "survivalism" and a theory of "compromise" regarding black culture, including religion and music. The theory of survival refers to traces of African culture in black America. It traces the persistence of "Africanisms" in black American culture in spite of all conscious and unconscious attempts to eradicate them.[3] The theory of compromise acknowledges the European influence on black American culture as well. The latter theory reconciles the opposing survivalist and nonsurvivalist theories. For example, numerous traits from English, French, Scottish, and Irish music have been used by black musicians. Kebede writes:

> The numerous French influences on black people are easily recognized in the creole culture of Louisiana and the West Indies; here, the hybridization of French and African elements is evident in the language (Créole), music, dance, religion, folklore, and other aspects of the culture.[4]

Specific examples of the carryover of African traits in black music support his survivalist claims. "Calls" and "cries" are offered as important "Africanisms" in black music. Since black slaves were forbidden, while working, to talk to one another, they used calls to communicate. In this way they converted speech to song. Kebede writes:

> They often consist of a variety of short messages that were sung solo to attract attention, to warn an inattentive friend at a distance of the approaching white overseer, to break a long monotonous silence, and to summon slaves, to work, to eat, or to gather.[5]

Calls represent an example of what the author calls "music migration." Calls in African American music derived from Africa were first sung in African dialects. In Africa, peasants melodically call to announce an emergency or spread news from village to village, to organize a work gang to farm the land of a sick neighbor, or just to convey greetings. These calls could travel long distances, over mountains and hills. The cultural migration of this form of music may be observed in communities like Haiti, Cuba, Trinidad, and Jamaica. In the United States calls are known as "hollers" and "whoopin'."[6]

Cries are used primarily to communicate messages. They express a deeply felt emotional experience, such as hunger, loneliness, or love sickness. Cries are half-sung and half-yelled. Kebede writes:

> Vocables are often intermixed in the text. The melodies are performed in a free and spontaneous style; they are often ornamented and employ

many African vocal devices, such as yodels, echo-like falsettos, tonal glides, embellished melismas, and microtonal inflections that are often impossible to indicate in European staff notation.[7]

The work song is another facet of African origins in black American music. Singing while at work was characteristic of the slaves. In sub-Saharan Africa men and women almost always sing while working. Even Albert Schweitzer, who was not very close to African culture despite his many years of work in Africa, came to appreciate the role of the work song. He at first considered Africans lazy, but he discovered they worked well when they sang. Slave masters did not object to slaves singing as long as they did their work. It was not long before American slave owners, too, observed that slaves worked harder when they sang. Furthermore, they saw that there was usually a lead singer who set the pace for the group. When there was a slave auction, singers with the strongest voices brought top prices.

The role of singing leader at work resembles that of the song leader or the preacher in the black church. The song leader must have a feel for the work being done. He or she must understand those with whom the work is being done and have the capacity to evoke the appropriate music and motor response for the group. Thus the work song of the slave had a direct relation to labor performed and the mood of the slaves. Even the sound of the work often accompanied the song. For example, the sound of the axe while cutting trees or chopping wood or the sound of chains in prison camp provides rhythmic background to work songs. Injustice, love, and other concerns with intense passion were often incorporated in black work songs.

"Long John" is one of the most representative of black American work songs. It has many versions and deals with a legendary character named Long John, who escaped from prison and obtained his freedom. The song seems to have a double meaning. Reference to the biblical John is instructive. Kebede writes:

It is sung responsorially: the chorus repeats each stanza, sung by the leader. The sound of axes, as the prisoners chop logs, provides an *ostinato* rhythm, a regularly recurring beat, in the background. Obviously, the melodic and rhythmic characteristics of the song, the vocal style, and the performance mannerisms of the singers are African derived. Only the language is Afro-American.[8]

Thus far we have been concerned with the African origin of black music in general, but there seems to be abundant evidence of the survival of African traits in all forms of black music.

The Prophethood of Black Believers

A Brief Natural History of Soul

The concept of "soul" is a descriptive index to the character of black music. It is perhaps more appropriate to describe soul than it is to define it. In a real sense black culture is full of soul. Therefore, to understand this quality of black culture is to gain a deeper understanding of black people. Soul is found in black religion as well as black music. Soul brings religion and music together in a powerful way.

LeRoi Jones in *Blues People* presents the idea that *blues* are the common denominator of black music. Jones sees a musical development that represents "the transmutation" of the African. At first Africans believed that their stay in the United States was temporary. When they discovered by force of circumstance that their plight was irreversible, they found a way to adjust to a hostile and oppressive environment. This reaction to the subhuman position imposed upon the African slaves led to the creation of a particular type of music, one which sprang from what Jones calls a blues attitude. Jones reasons that African cultures, the retention of some parts of these cultures in America, produced the American Negro as a new race.[9] Using music as the prime referent to this change and blues as an index to it, Jones observes: "It is a native American music, the product of the black man in this country. . . . Blues could not exist if the African captives had not become American captives."[10]

Jones views the social context and human reaction as prime factors in musical development. This view has a lot of value as we seek to understand the soul quality of black music and black religion as they commingle. When we look for the roots of soul, we must look to the plantations, especially to the cotton fields of Dixie. Here we discover that Africans carried with them many elements of an African heritage. Not the least of these were music and rhythm. Phyl Garland points out the importance of rhythm in African music and its derivatives:

> The distinguishing characteristic of African music is its polyrhythmic nature, the quality whereby different rhythms are piled one on top of the other and played simultaneously and somehow made to fall into place in constantly shifting patterns. As a simple experiment, one might try beating 4/4 with one hand and 3/4 with the other. Now consider the effect when four or five such rhythms are played together while deliberately placed accents add yet another quality to this woven fabric of tempos, as is common in West Africa, from which American blacks came. A much simpler but similar use of rhythm is to be found in jazz and much of popular music today, where extra beats or accents are placed in all sections of the spaces between the regular beats.[11]

Antiphony, an exchange between a leader and the chorus or audience, is characteristic. This pattern is common in black as well as West African music. It is manifest in the talked-shout-sung sermon in a black Baptist or Pentecostal church. This style can be compared with the form of classic blues, in which an observation is stated in music, repeated in a slightly altered form, and followed by a line of comment on the initial statement. Often an instrumentalist in the band injects "comments." In a jazz band, the repetitive ensemble brass may answer the call of a saxophonist, trumpeter, pianist, or vocalist. Recent examples are found in the music of Ray Charles or Aretha Franklin with the Sweet Inspirations shouting behind her.[12]

Melville J. Herskovits, in his landmark anthropological study *The Myth of the Negro Past*, has pinpointed two salient characteristics of African and Afro-American music. He emphasizes the "ubiquity" of the drum in African music and the corresponding prominence of rhythm in black music of the Americas. Herskovits noted the close integration between song and dance in Afro-cultures, the tendency of audiences or choruses to accompany musicians with hand clapping and to "dance a song" in both sacred and secular music, and the widespread reliance on improvisation. There is, he observed, an emphasis on antiphony:

> The pattern whereby the statement of a theme is repeated by a chorus, or a short choral pause is balanced as a refrain against a longer melodic line sung by the soloist, is fundamental and has been commented on by all who have heard Negroes sing in Africa or elsewhere. The relationship of the melody to an accompanying rhythm—carried on by drums, rattles, sticks beaten one against another, hand clapping, or short nonmusical cries is also [characteristic of this music]. So prominent is the rhythmic element in Negro music that this music as ordinarily conceived relegates the element of melody to second place.[13]

According to Herskovits, then, the pivotal characteristic of music in Afro-cultures is rhythm. Melody and harmony are present, but rhythm takes the high ground—it is the controlling category.

The African elements provide a foundation for the development of black music in the Americas. The development, however, was closely linked to events in the New World. For example, there was a different pattern in areas outside the United States. In the Latin-Catholic colonies of the Caribbean there was a more limited cultural exchange than in the British-Protestant colonies of North America.[14] Herskovits also sees the close association between black slaves and slave owners as significant in the U.S. South. In Haiti, for example, there was a successful independence movement against the French minority. Thus the drum-heavy

The Prophethood of Black Believers

ritualistic sounds of Haiti are quite close to the African originals. This explains why the highly rhythmic dances called the conga, rumba, mambo, and cha-cha, all basically African, did not originate in Virginia, but in Cuba. Cuba was dominated by Spain, a nation whose music already reflected the influence of the Moorish invasion. The popular Spanish dance, the flamenco, reflects African influence with its rhythmic clapping and stomping improvizations.

In the United States the "Caribbean style" of music found its most dramatic expression in New Orleans, a French colony. There the Roman Catholic culture had more tolerance for traditional African culture than the British-Puritan parts of the United States. The invasion of New Orleans by the purer African music of the Caribbean may explain why jazz developed there.[15]

Even in parts of the United States dominated by slavery and Puritanism, the slave clung to some element of the indigenous music from Africa. This is perhaps because in Africa art is not separated from life. Music, therefore, is interwoven into activities of life. Garland writes:

In Africa, music is one of the means by which cultural traditions are passed on from one generation to another. Through music, old men and women voice their philosophical attitudes and indoctrinate the young with the principles to which they should adhere. Through music, legends of history are transmitted, warriors are incited to fight. It is in Africa, for example, that the talking drum, which can be used to convey specific messages, is found. Then, too, music is used in connection with toil.[16]

At the heart of black music is rhythm, and music is at the center of life for Africans and their descendants in the New World. Music is also at the heart of African and Afro-American religious experience. Blacks carry the rhythm of their music with them to church.

Black Sacred Music and Social Change

The title of this section is suggested by the subtitle of Wyatt Tee Walker's book, *Somebody's Calling My Name: Black Sacred Music and Social Change*. According to Walker, there are three central components of worship in the black church's worship: music, preaching, and praying. There is no agreement as to which takes first place, preaching or singing. Preaching and singing go together. Great preaching is supported by outstanding music.[17] Most black churches that are effective in ministries to black people have outstanding choirs. If excellent music is supported by outstanding preaching, the church is likely to be well-attended and motivated for a significant witness in the community.

Outstanding music attracts black people from all backgrounds and of all ages. Music is especially attractive to black youth, whether male or female. It is a force in black life that levels classes and has an intergenerational flow. Older people and their grandchildren are often seen following the rhythm of great music in the black church at worship. In the sacred experience of black songs in worship, black people become one. All are caught up into a true fellowship of believers. Music has the power to inspire and unite in the context of worship.

Black music has led a whole generation of black people, especially college and university students, back to church. In the search for African roots, they have discovered black music and the religious content of much of such music. Many black studies programs have generated outstanding "gospel choirs." Many of these young people have returned to church. Other gospel choirs have been organized that consist mainly of young people, men and women in their late teens and early twenties. In some cases black sacred music has helped young black people overcome a crisis of identity as they have discovered their African ancestry and their Afro-American past. In some cases, they have also found a deep commitment to the Christian faith. Some have been led to an ordained ministry. The potential of black sacred music is yet to be realized and fully understood.

We need to give some serious thought to the power of sacred music to attract black youth, its leveling effects between the black masses and classes, and its ability to create a fellowship where people of all ages become united in worship. There is more happening than feeling or the search for roots. We are reminded by Wyatt Tee Walker that black sacred music rooted in the African heritage has the potential to inspire a ministry of social change:

> The presence of the music of the Black religious tradition has served as a device to fire and fuel most of the efforts, large and small, for the liberation of the oppressed personally and collectively. . . . It has been the churches peopled with the masses which have retained the music and worship style that is identifiably Africa linked and which have been in the forefront of much of the struggle for liberation.[18]

If we are to put the "radicalism" or "protest" dimensions of black music back into worship, we will need to reintroduce the *spirituals*. Unfortunately, many of our black youth in the church do not have an acquaintance with this rich musical form. They have been brought up on gospel but have no knowledge or appreciation for the spirituals and their strong message of liberation.

Spirituals carry a twofold message. Spirituals cultivate "black spirituality." They also nurture our personal faith, speaking of life and death. Their message is profound in a therapeutic or priestly sense. Spirituals contain "the balm in Gilead" that makes the wounded whole.

The one person who contributed most to the appreciation of the deep spirituality of the spirituals was Howard Thurman. During recent years his contribution to our understanding of the black religious experience, including the spirituals, has been overshadowed by the "political" focus of black theology. Now there is some indication that Thurman is being rediscovered. On the inner aspect of faith this is a great gain. As we look at the power of black music it is essential that we reflect on Thurman's interpretation of black faith through the spirituals. Thurman wrote a great deal and he left an abundance of material in sermons and meditations.[19]

The one brief example from Thurman given here is a reflection on a refrain of the black spiritual "There Is a Balm in Gilead":

> There is a balm in Gilead,
> to make the spirit whole.
> There is a balm in Gilead,
> to heal the sin-sick soul.

Thurman explains that slaves, as they studied the Book of Jeremiah, realized that the prophet had become despondent. Jeremiah was discouraged over external events in the life of Israel, but he was also spiritually depressed and tortured. He cried out, "Is there no balm in Gilead? Is no physician there?" This is a question, Thurman asserts, that was not raised to God or Israel; it was a question raised by Jeremiah's entire life. He was searching his soul. The prophet was engaged in self-reflection. He pondered inwardly, "there must be a balm in Gilead." Thurman writes: "The relentless winnowing of his own bitter experience has laid bare his soul to the end that he is brought face to face with the very ground and core of his own faith."[20]

According to Thurman, the slave who created this spiritual caught the mood of Jeremiah's question. The slave did an amazing thing. He "straightened the question mark in Jeremiah's sentence into an exclamation point: He sang, 'There is a balm in Gilead!' Here is a note of creative triumph."[21]

This resolve of the black slave, for Thurman, was more than a defense mechanism; it explains how blacks, through profound religious belief, were able to survive the slave experience. They had discovered hope against hope. They gained the profound insight that the contradictions of life are not ultimate. And because the contradictions of life are not ultimate, there is always the growing edge of hope. This is so even in the midst of "the most barren and most tragic circumstances."[22]

Thurman goes on to explain his view:

There is something in the spirit of man that knows that dualism, however binding, runs out, exhausts itself, and leaves a core of assurance that the ultimate destiny of man is good. This becomes the raw material of all hope, and is one of the tap-roots of religious faith for the human spirit. When it applies to the individual and becomes the norm of human relationships, a new sense of the ethical significance of life becomes manifest.[23]

Thurman's unusual insight into the meaning of the spirituals has present efficacy. A black woman who had studied the writings of Thurman with me in seminary later contacted me when she was under great financial and intellectual stress in graduate school. I reminded her of Thurman's assertion: "Remember that the contradictions of life are never final!" She later reported that reflecting upon that statement, putting it in the context of Thurman's whole corpus, and personalizing its meaning, gave her the strength not only to continue but also to complete her doctoral studies with distinction.

There is abundant evidence in the study of the spirituals that their rediscovery is needed. Their message is therapeutic. They have a vital priestly message. They have the means to empower black people to endure the suffering and hardship that racism inflicts upon them. They also provide faith and hope to confront the burdens and misfortunes of human life itself. The spirituals are a musical tradition we need to reclaim for the sake of art and for the purpose of faith to confront life as it is. They remind us that there is a "balm in Gilead, to make the spirit whole."

The healing dimension of black religion is not unrelated to the liberating or political aspect. The spirituals have a message of liberation, as well. This James H. Cone lifts up in his *Spirituals and Blues*.[24] Both the liberation and the personal-spiritual aspects of the message of the spirituals have a this-worldly significance. There can be no political freedom without psychological freedom. Thus it was proper that black *consciousness* and *power* were interfaced. The spirituals, therefore, prepare us for social and political activism.

Miles Mark Fisher, in *Negro Slave Songs*, provided a double interpretation of the spirituals that laid the groundwork for use of this form of music by Cone in his black theology of liberation. According to Fisher, the spirituals were both this-worldly and otherworldly in their message. The slaves used "veiled" language in producing this form of music. Fisher, in studying the Bible, especially the books of Daniel and Revelation, gleaned an insight that he applied to black slavery. Just as these biblical documents had a different message for the oppressors and the oppressed, the spirituals also spoke to the slaves and to slave owners with different messages. To the slave owners their message appeared to be otherworldly, while to the slave the message was one of freedom—for example escape to Canada by way of underground railroad. The following are examples:

> I want to go to Canaan,
> I want to go to Canaan,
> I want to go to Canaan,
> To meet 'em at de comin' day.

and,

> O, Jordan bank was a great old bank!
> Dere ain't but one more river to cross.
> . . . .
> Dere's a hill on my left, and he catch on my right,
> Dere ain't but one more river to cross.[25]

These spirituals are selected as representative of those that seem to clearly bear a twofold message as described above. The biblical message provides the backdrop for either a religious message or a liberation message in relation to earthly freedom by "going to Canaan" or "crossing Jordan." Thus, it is not necessary to choose between those scholars like Benjamin E. Mays, who derives a compensatory message from the spirituals, and Fisher, who gets a double meaning from this music. The spirituals seem to be open to either view. This author prefers a balanced interpretation in which great meaning can be derived from the spirituals in many directions. The spirituals do speak of life and death, they provide spiritual nurture for those on the edge of survival, they look to heaven for release from the burdens of earthly life, and they provide a vital message for those seeking liberation from earthly forms of oppression, including slavery and racism. Thus, the spirituals provide a rich heritage in black music that the black church must use again and again in its mission and ministry. Each generation of blacks must be taught the spirituals for their own nurture and growth in the very art of living in a difficult and troubled world.

Toward a Theomusicology

Jon Michael Spencer's term *theomusicology* provides an umbrella under which to bring together black music, black church theology, and ministry.[26] In that we have been addressing issues related to the "ministry of black music," a discussion of theomusicology seems an appropriate way to bring our thoughts together as we conclude this chapter.

Thus far, there has been inadequate theological reflection on the theological message conveyed through black sacred music. There is a distinct need for black religious scholarship to provide a sound message to be communicated through the powerful medium of black music. We are often caught up in the medium and neglect to evaluate critically the message being communicated through musical renditions in black churches. As we have seen, black sacred music in the past has been able to say something of great theological significance to black people in their struggles. We need constantly to examine the music of the past that has been so helpful to spiritual growth and racial uplift. This is true of hymns as well as of the spirituals. We need to consider gospel music with the same critical outlook. What may appear to be only secular forms of music—for example, blues, rap, and jazz—need to be examined as art forms that may be a receptacle for a powerful theological message.

Black people are a religious people. At the same time, we are a musical people. We have already seen this combination in our heritage. It is likewise in our church tradition. Now we are challenged to take the theological criticism and interpretation of black music seriously. Musical talent alone will not suffice. It must be informed and guided by informed biblical, theological, and ethical reflection that will nurture aright our black congregants.

I shall separate *protest* and *praise* for the sake of analysis. In black sacred music, which, like black religious experience, is holistic, protest and praise are two sides of the same coin, so to speak. Sometimes both protest and praise appear in the same song. Which dimension receives priority will depend on the purpose for which the music is being sung or the meaning ascribed to the words. In order to undergird my discussion theologically, I shall draw on works by two brothers who have contributed to black theology, James Cone and Cecil Cone. In *Spirituals and Blues*, James H. Cone uses his liberation-from-oppression formula at the heart of his theological project to interpret "spirituals" and "blues."[27] A fringe benefit of his study is that it demonstrates the close kinship between secular and sacred music in the black experience. The mood and rhythm in one saturates the other. The message may be different but the medium is quite similar. But our concern goes deeper. Cone is thinking "theologically" about black music. Since his theological outlook is "political," he finds an abundance of protest content in both forms of black music. In the spirit of W. E. B. Du Bois, the spirituals are "sorrow songs." Thus the mood of these music forms is directed to the suffering and bondage of blacks in slavery and in "the shadow of slavery." Freedom from racist oppression is the message of the black song. James Cone found what he was looking for not just because he was looking, but because, as we have seen, the black music tradition undergirds his theological quest and illustrates the same.

James Cone, Gayraud Wilmore, and several other leading black religious interpreters have made the case for the "radicalism" of black religion for several centuries in this country. Thus James Cone is on course as he traces this protest tradition through the black music forms he has selected for his study. There are solid biblical, historical, and ethical warrants for his important political interpretation of these forms of black music.

One example will suffice, based upon black theology's appropriation of the exodus story. Almost from the time blacks were introduced to the Bible, they discovered that this biblical account was symbolic of their own bondage and the desire to be free. Thus the biblical summons "Let my people go!" had a direct message for black people. The leadership of Moses also became a model for religiously inspired black leaders, men and women. Harriet Tubman as well as Marcus Garvey were known by the name Moses. The exodus conveyed a profound message of liberation, filled with profound theological context. It portrayed the message of liberation from oppression. The spiritual "Go Down Moses" has always communicated a message of liberation from oppression for black people. This is a political message of protest as well as a spiritual message of hope.

Cecil Cone in *Identity-Crisis in Black Theology* lifts up an aspect of black religion/theology different from that discussed by James Cone. Cecil is critical of all black theologians who take their departure from "black power," including James Cone and this writer. He sees in black religion with its African roots evidence of a joyous celebration of the sovereignty of God. The omnipotence of God is central to the understanding of the divine in both African and Afro-American religion. Worship consists of submission to the ultimate will of God. Worship, according to Cecil Cone, is full of praise. He writes: "Black worship is the community celebrating their encounter of freedom."[28]

If we, therefore, approach black theology in light of Cecil Cone's outlook, we will emphasize *praise* rather than *protest* as the most characteristic element in black sacred music. It seems to me that this will point more in the direction of gospel music as the best means of expression. Let us now turn briefly to the black musical form called gospel.

Jon Michael Spencer has devoted a chapter of his book *Protest and Praise* to gospel[29] in a well-researched and informative discussion. He has used the typologies of H. Richard Niebuhr in *Christ and Culture* as a framework.[30] In this often quoted work, Niebuhr relates Jesus Christ to human culture by using five types: (1) Christ against culture, (2) Christ of culture, (3) Christ above culture, (4) Christian culture in paradox, and (5) Christ the transformer of culture. Spencer's use of Niebuhr's typologies is apropos since he views gospel music as Christocentric.

After looking critically at several interpretations of black gospel music, Spencer concludes that the assessment of Louis Charles Harvey is most significant theologically. In his essay "Black Gospel Music and Black Theology," Harvey reports that his study of seventeen hundred gospel songs revealed that nearly a third were centered on the person of Jesus Christ. Upon this discovery of the Christocentrism of gospel, Harvey based his thesis that the most characteristic statement about Jesus Christ is that he is "everything." He is *friend*, *protector*, and *liberator*. In other words, Jesus is regarded as the answer to the problems of black life.[31]

Spencer assumes, using Niebuhr's typologies, that gospel music is essentially anticultural. Gospel focuses upon a Christ who is against culture. This emphasis is traced through the history of gospel in three historic periods. The first period Spencer calls "Transitional Gospel" (1900–1930). Representatives of this period are Charles Albert Tindley, Methodist, and Charles Price Jones, Holiness. This is also designated the "Pre-Gospel Era." The "Traditional" period, or the "Golden Age of Gospel" (1930–1969), was dominated by Thomas A. Dorsey, a Baptist songwriter influenced by Tindley. Dorsey, and other musical composers of the Golden Age of Gospel, transformed the congregational *gospel hymn* of the transitional period into the solo, quartet, and choral *gospel song* of the latter period. Dorsey's time-honored masterpiece is "Precious Lord, Take My Hand."

Finally, we come to the "Contemporary Period," or the "Modern Gospel Era" (1969–present). This period is dominated by artists of the Church of God in Christ. Edwin Hawkins, Walter Hawkins, Andrae Crouch, and the Clark Sisters are among the leaders of this movement. The era started with the Edwin Hawkins Singers' recorded arrangement of the old Baptist hymn "O Happy Day" in 1969. Spencer sees a glimpse of a Christ who is the transformer of culture in Edwin Hawkins. Jesus is said to be savior of this world as well as the next. Hawkins, through the ministry of song, exhorts the followers of Christ to apply their love-transformed vocations toward the conversion of this world.[32] According to this songwriter, if you want the world to be "a better place," you should try love and peace.[33]

According to Spencer, gospel music has certain fundamental themes: cross-bearing, crown-wearing, and crown-wearing in the course of cross-bearing. The power symbols that enable believers to carry out the will of God are the "name" and "blood" of Jesus. "Praise" includes the

The Prophethood of Black Believers

aspects of celebration and thanksgiving. These are the means whereby believers attest to *power*. The theme of *salvation* comprises three subcategories: witness to the unsaved, the saving deeds of Jesus, and the believer's quest for the church's affirmation of his or her experience of salvation. The theme of *struggle* includes such aspects as trouble, battle, danger, fear, judgment, desperation, determination, and steadfastness.[34]

Henry H. Mitchell and Nicholas Cooper-Lewter, in *Soul Theology*, provide some noteworthy theological reflections on gospel and other forms of black music. They observe that themes of God and humanity are lifted up in black sacred music. They list the following: (1) the providence of God, (2) the justice of God, (3) the majesty and omnipotence of God, (4) the omniscience of God, (5) the goodness of God and creation, (6) the grace of God, (7) the equality of persons, (8) the uniqueness of persons: identity, (9) the family of God and humanity, and (10) the steadfastness or long-suffering of persons. The first six themes reflect on God, but the last four focus on humanity. They therefore conclude that black people intuitively select songs that provide them with nourishment and therapeutic affirmation they need to endure.[35]

It is, I think, correct for Spencer to see gospel music, especially in its present form, as problematic. It does engage the concerns of black people as an oppressed group. But its main emphasis is to point to heaven rather than to the earth. Spencer seems mainly concerned, in his final critique, about gospel not meeting the test of pluralism. It has a partial vision. It does not speak of Jesus as Reconciler, nor is it concerned about reconciliation.[36] In reference to black people and their this-worldly needs and concerns, it does not appear to address sufficiently the theme of *liberation*. Thus far it does not appear at all informed by the main thrust of the black theology movement. This seems to indicate the need for a serious encounter between black theologians and black musicologists. Since both are concerned about ministry and worship in black churches, this encounter is long overdue.

Summary

This exploration of black sacred music has reflected mainly upon two forms, spiritual and gospel. Other forms of black music also influence ministry in the black churches. For instance, hymns are transformed by the black music tradition with its African roots. Rap music has real potential. It is popular among the young, and it could be a receptacle for ethical and religious values for the new generations. In its various forms black music is a powerful medium of communication in the black church. It needs and deserves serious theological reflection and criticism if it is to serve its purpose in the ministry and mission of black churches.

Spirituals reach deep into our heritage and are open to diverse interpretations. The message of the spirituals is multidimensional. We have to look at them in reference to both their deep spirituality and their protest potential, as represented by Howard Thurman and James Cone. Spirituality in Thurman does not exclude social criticism, while protest in Cone does not denounce spirituality. What we have is a difference in emphasis. We have also viewed gospel music in its historical development as being countercultural and perhaps too otherworldly. However, we have also observed that in the case of Edwin Hawkins, there is a this-worldly focus, as well. The potential for development in the direction of social transformation is there. A very productive possibility in theomusicology would be for black theologians and black musicologists to combine their insights and skills toward the empowerment of black gospel music. Some of this is happening through the contribution of Wyatt Tee Walker. May his tribe increase.

11

Faith and Praxis: What About the Future?

WE ARE NOW INTO THE LAST DECADE OF THE twentieth century. This is a time of rapid change. All our goals seem to be moving targets. Whatever we say, do, or think needs to be dynamic rather than static. However, beneath these obvious changes, something must remain constant. There always needs to be a point of reference in those things of permanent value as we chart our future. We must examine the best in our past for the sake of the noble future.

Alvin Toffler, a futurologist, has produced three best sellers, *Future Shock*, *Third Wave*, and *Power Shift*. In all of these volumes he has described knowledge, wealth, violence, and power on the edge of the twenty-first century. His volumes are both challenging and disturbing. This is especially true for "rootless" people. In *Power Shift*, Toffler startles us with this statement: "Power is shifting at so astonishing a rate that world leaders are being swept along by events rather than imposing order on them."[1]

Toffler asserts that a "power shift" does not merely transfer power, it transforms it. Some power shifting is normal, yet only rarely does an entire "globe-girding system" of power fly apart. It is even rarer, Toffler asserts, that all rules of the power game change at once and the very nature of power is revolutionized. Power that defines us as individuals and as nations is itself being redefined.[2]

Toffler powerfully assesses the future and its challenges. We must not be overawed by the challenge of the future. In one sense, we must seek to be all the more securely anchored in the faith of the Christian tradition. Our knowledge of and orientation in our heritage must become a sure and steadfast foundation. When changes are as rapid and as radical as they seem, we have a need for a secure place to stand. There is a great need for permanence amid change, if life is to have meaning and direction.

Another way of stating our concern is to assert that in a fundamental sense, life is dialectical. There is a tension between past and present and future. A useable past is already merged into the present and it is challenged by the pull of the future. Our concern here is with the resources of the Christian faith that have sustained the life of black people through what Dr. Martin Luther King Jr. described as "the dark night of suffering." We have recalled how blacks as slaves reinterpreted the Christian faith to find meaning in a life of bondage. We recall how blacks through more than four hundred years discovered in the combination of African roots and black faith experience (informed by Christianity) a means not merely to survive, but to prevail. This hope against hope woven out of our experience of oppression and liberation has brought us as a people to the edge of the twenty-first century.

Much depends now upon how we are able to negotiate our future amid the cataclysmic changes we face. While rapid and shattering changes are taking place throughout our world, the focus of this chapter will be on *localization*. Although I am intensely concerned with what is happening in Russia, Eastern Europe, South Africa, and Haiti, among other places, there has to be a focus somewhere. For this study, it is upon black America. What we are able to say and do for the benefit of the uplift of black people will have a ripple effect around the globe. Thus we can move from the particular to the universal. The leaders of our nation have discovered of late that "the new world order" cannot be established while ignoring "the bread-and-butter issues" here at home.

Ideological Reflections

As I conclude this volume, I am aware that the ideologies upon which we must reflect are many and the issues we face are almost endless. This is indeed a time of crisis. Yet a time of crisis is also a time of decision and opportunity. Multiple challenges face those who minister to black people. Black churches still have unlimited potential in offering a liberating and healing ministry on behalf of black people. This includes the "haves" and the "have-nots."

Black people have a tendency to overlook the importance of rigorous thinking. Few black scholars have become philosophers. There is a conviction that abstract thinking is a waste of valuable time better spent in action. For many blacks, the social sciences, for example, have seemed more to the point. Those of us who have been given to rigorous thinking often find ourselves feeling useless in the struggle for racial justice. After careful reflection we often feel that we are without the knowledge or the means to communicate to the masses or to effect empirical change.

However, again and again we observe that "ideas have consequences," sometimes constructive and at other times destructive. Behind most movements, there are powerful ideas. Sometimes these ideas are clear and obvious. At other times they are hidden and subtle. For example, "integration" and "nationalism" are two broad ideas that have been central to blacks in their long struggle for racial justice. This has been powerfully discussed in a recent book by James H. Cone, *Martin and Malcolm and America*.[3]

These ideologies have been around a long time. They constantly reappear in black history. They are often embodied in the life and activity of an activist who is also a thinker, like Booker T. Washington or W. E. B. Du Bois. In addition, these ideas inform a movement such as the NAACP or the Urban League.[4] In black history no less than in Marxism, ideas have powerful consequences. We need, therefore, to be critical in the assessment of such ideas. We need to sort them out, think them through, and make constructive use of the ideologies that are suitable for our liberation from racist oppression.

Racism itself is an ideology. Racism has serious consequences in the life of black people. It is based upon a belief that whites are superior to blacks. Reasons are given. The theory is argued and evidence is provided to establish the racial superiority of whites over blacks. At times so-called "scientific" evidence is provided to establish the credibility of the "racist ideology" of white superiority. For example, the controversy over intelligence testing refuses to die. Behind this controversy is an ideology, namely, the genetic inferiority of black people. Scholars like Arthur R. Jensen and others sponsor this ideology.[5]

What is more devastating to black youth is "neo-racism." It is not manifest in an obvious form. It is hidden, subtle, and frequently unconscious. It is often undetected by the victim. It is, however, the more destructive because of its insidious character. Neo-racism is nationwide and it is powerfully present in structural and institutional manifestations. Recently I was stunned when I engaged in a public forum on racism. A black woman deeply involved in drug addiction said sincerely that she did not even know that racism existed. She was trapped in a subculture of poverty and woeful deprivation. She blamed herself for all that had happened to her. It was not possible to communicate to her the relationship of racism to her tragic condition.

The point is that the ideology of race is so powerful that it persists by taking different forms of expression. As it does so we need to be able to recognize it, analyze it, and interpret it. Only thus may we be in a position to resist and overcome its negative influence upon each new generation. This is as true of white youth as it is of black youth. Both the victims and beneficiaries of racist ideology need to know it for what it is in order to overcome its deadly power. The fallout from racism is very destructive to all blacks today. Racism could lead America to self-destruction.

This lack of awareness of racism on the part of black members of the underclass is matched by blacks who in their personal life have ascended to great heights in the corporate, educational, or political sectors of American society. This can be seen in theological schools as well. Upon being accepted on pietistic or spiritual terms as apparently equal, black seminarians may easily overlook the absence of black faculty, administrators, and trustees in their seminary community. Not being informed by black consciousness and black power, they are not even aware of the ideology of racism operating in their midst. One such black student, addressing a senior class, was so uplifted by the experience he had had in an obviously "racist" community that he vowed he would never be able to pastor a black church. This illustrates the insidious force of neo-racism. Wherever blacks find themselves, they must never lose their critical judgment. Racism at any place, under any guise, must always be identified and opposed. Racism in all of its forms destroys, even kills, black people. We must not allow racism to "hide behind the cross." As blacks rub shoulders with white Christians, insofar as racism is concerned, they must not allow sentimental love to replace what Reinhold Niebuhr described as "the pushing and shoving justice."

We could discuss "black power" and/or "black consciousness," "non-violent direct action," and "Ethiopianism" as ideologies. These have been much discussed over several decades. However, there is a more recent ideology that has yet to be fully examined. *Afrocentrism* has had a powerful effect both at the intellectual and mass levels of the black community. In fact, the force of this idea will not be denied. Black ministers and churches are slow to comprehend the full influence of new ideas. Some of this inattention is related to the emphasis upon survival issues in black life. Also the institutes and convocations that attract large numbers of black religious leaders focus mainly on Bible study and preaching. Ideologies like Afrocentricity are dismissed as too abstract to be considered. Yet Afrocentricity will soon strike the black minister and congregations with full force. This ideology will be a great challenge to the business-as-usual outlook in black churches. Yet it will offer a golden opportunity for the mission and ministry of black churches, especially to the underclass.

Afrocentrism will have great impact on churches because of its current impact upon education in the public schools of urban America. This ideology is taking black educators and students by storm. One of the philosophers of this movement is Molefi Kete Asante, who is head of

The Prophethood of Black Believers

Temple University's African American Studies Department. Asante defines Afrocentricity as follows:

> Afrocentricity is a philosophy based on centering concepts, ideas, and thoughts in an African context. One dimension of the philosophy is the perspective of viewing Africans as subjects rather than objects, that is as human agents operating on our own terms. In Afrocentricity the idea of African is not limited to the continent of Africa but exists wherever people of African descent exist. . . . Afrocentricity is not a black version of Eurocentrism which has become an ethnocentric view because it places the white experience as a universal experience and downgrades other cultural experiences.[6]

Asante further explains this ideology by asserting that it promotes unity and cohesion in American society by giving African people an appreciation of their past that may enhance their respect for other cultures. It provides them with the ability to bring an owned perspective to the assembly of American cultures. It is said to be a positive outlook. In a word, it leads black people to be the subjects rather than the objects of history.[7] Afrocentricity is another example of ideas that have consequences in the life of a people. If Asante is the philosopher of Afrocentricity, Asa Hilliard, of Georgia State University, may be said to be the educational expert. Through workshops, tracts, and tours, Hilliard has introduced the concept of Afrocentricity to many black teachers throughout the nation. When black teachers and students are imbibing a powerful ideology, black ministers and congregations had better take notice.

The task of the black theologians, as well as other religious scholars, will be to reflect upon this ideology and interpret it. They must understand it to such an extent that they will be able to tone it down, communicate it, and make it practical for use by those who minister to black people on all levels. Every ideology may not be acceptable to black believers in the church of Jesus Christ. When an ideology is mainly destructive, we must be able to make the case for its rejection. Happily, Afrocentricity can have positive value. It should be presented in this way with thoughtful conviction on the part of the black theologian.

Cain Felder, a New Testament scholar at the Howard University Divinity School, argues that Afrocentricity has the potential to take us beyond where black theology has taken us during the last twenty years. It gives us an appreciation of our noble African ancestry before slavery. In other words, blacks can now value their heritage, not as one of oppression in the United States, but as one of noble ancestry before their American sojourn and, indeed, independent of it. If this is so, it will help us overcome one of the worst psychological scars of racism, and that is the inferiority complex of blackness. This insight alone is worthy of long and serious reflection and application. If through education in the family, school, and church, we can pass on this lesson of self-respect and pride of peoplehood, we will improve the promise of the next generation of black people.

The challenge of pluralism in the form of multiculturalism is our next ideological concern. It is important to read the signs of the times, but it is also necessary to know the space in which one stands. Thus this concern may be described more in terms of localization than globalization. The present writer, as well as many black religious thinkers/leaders, is ultimately a universalist. We must embrace a common humanity, especially for the sake of peace. However, we must not attempt to leap to the universal. Universalism can be a meaningless abstraction. The only concrete way to pursue the universal is through the particular. By particularity I do not mean a rugged provincialism. What is important is how blacks and their churches can become effective in their mission in the context of the ethnic pluralism in the United States.

When we raise this issue, the term "African American" can have real meaning. Lifting up the African ancestry dimension can have something to say about the black American's place amid others who have come to these shores from other parts of the world. The term African American may be more appropriate now than it has ever been since so many of those who are newcomers to the nation are nonwhite ethnics who often find themselves living in communities already populated by blacks. Often, especially in the case of Hispanics, they must seek to forge a new community in which they may live together in peace and cooperation. This is a situation somewhat different from the earlier influx of European immigrants, who were mainly cousins to white Americans. Those who are now coming from third-world countries are not kinfolk, they are total strangers. A great challenge for African Americans is to find a constructive way to forge community with the strangers in their midst.

Before we pursue this line of thought further, we need to say that we must not forget our "blackness" and what this implies. We have four hundred years of history in the United States. We came in chains. We did not come voluntarily nor did we come as political refugees; we came mainly as slaves. We provided more than two hundred and fifty years of free labor. We fought in all the wars. We helped to build railroads and establish this nation as the greatest industrial power in world history. Yet we have been oppressed in one way or another throughout our sojourn. In a profound sense "blackness" sums up this experience as no other designation does. Thus the ideologies of Afrocentricity and African Americanism say something that needs to be said, but they do not preempt the meaning of blackness that sums up the total experience of

African Americans in the United States. We are African people in that we share a common ancestry. At the same time we are "American" in the unique sense described briefly above.

Having made this clarification of the sense in which use of the appellation "African American" can open up conversation with other so-called hyphenated Americans, we briefly suggest how the black churches can meet the challenge of ministry and mission amid a growing multiculturalism.

Black churches in their educational ministries can do much to develop this sense of multiculturalism. Some urban public school systems are already moving forward with this agenda. Public school teachers are struggling with Afrocentricity and multiculturalism at the same time. Their educative insights are transferable to our churches. Some black churches are developing Saturday schools. Two examples are New Shiloh Baptist Church in Baltimore and Zion Baptist Church in Philadelphia. These Saturday schools in black churches could be used to educate members of all ages in interethnic and cross-cultural studies. For example, classes in Spanish could be taught. These can be supported by people-to-people visits and fellowship. The alternative will be bloody confrontation between two oppressed ethnic groups. The powers that be like to set the weak against the weak. In the interest of survival, the weak may fight each other over the crumbs that fall from the master's table. A better way would be to forge an understanding with each other, uniting forces to liberate all of the oppressed.

The educative process should be supported by worship experiences together. There should be opportunities for Bible study, cross-cultural studies, family visits, and even cross-cultural tours abroad, which would provide an immersion experience for blacks in other cultures. Theological and ethical reflection, of an interethnic nature, should take place on the leadership level, including lay men, women, and youth. The more profound the encounter becomes, the deeper the meaning of the interethnic experience. The real payoff may come in social, economic, and political benefits for those involved in these significant exchanges. For instance, in cases where the combined vote of blacks and Hispanics could change the balance of power toward humanization, it would be better to cooperate than to split the vote. Splitting the vote would open the way for a politician insensitive to the needs of both oppressed groups to sweep into office. When this happens the bitterness and alienation of blacks against Hispanics is likely to increase. What we have said concerning Hispanics could be said regarding Koreans, Africans (from Africa), or Asians moving into established black neighborhoods. We now face a situation where black churches will need to broaden their ministerial missions to involve the multiculturalism in their midst.

This new challenge must be met in such a way as not to abandon the implications of the civil rights and black power movements. Thus as we seek to understand what we are to do in this time of multiculturalism, we must affirm for each new generation the meaning of "blackness." Black Theology remains a very important project for the black church. Black theologians, biblical scholars, and others must move into this new reality and provide direction for ministers and lay people alike.

Black Theological Reflection on Praxis

The term "praxis" is difficult to translate into English. It is used here because of its powerful message from Latin American liberation theology. This movement in Latin America has made its impact felt upon theology worldwide. In most of theological history, theology has used philosophy, mainly metaphysics, as an instrument for interpretation. Even Process Theology depends upon a neoclassical metaphysics, distilled from Alfred North Whitehead, as a framework for theological discourse and reflection. The Latin American liberation theologians have used Marxist analysis, but in spirit they have turned the theological method upside down. They have moved from the social reality to theological reflection. Action in solidarity with the oppressed poor is prior to theological reflection on the faith held by the poor. Compare this approach, for example, with the rigorous logic of Paul Tillich as he developed his systematic theology. Thus much of the spirit if not the substance of black theology is inspired by dialogue with Latin American liberation theology.

Both theologies are at their best when they are developed in solidarity with the oppressed. Black theology is at its best as "church theology." It is a theology for ministry. In a word, it is a "practicing" theology, a theology for active witnessing in the world among blacks as well as other peoples, groups. Its source is the living faith and lifestyle of black believers. The time has come for a greater emphasis upon "echoes from the field." Those who have laid a foundation in research and reflection need now to be good listeners as they hear the issues and questions from those who seek to be Christian in the midst of social, economic, and political oppression based upon race. It is one thing to be white and poor—it is another thing to be *black* and poor. For instance, one reason poor whites and blacks are unable to unite is the superiority complex of many poor whites (based on racism). This attitude makes poor whites feel superior to all blacks regardless of the achievements of any and all black persons.

Black theology for praxis must deal with the harsh realities of black life in the United States. To deal with reality is better than to harbor romantic notions about the racial situation. As long as we have parents who teach their children to hate blacks, Jews, and others, we have a serious problem with racism not just for the present but also for the future. Recently a director of the Ku Klux Klan had his daughter and his young granddaughter on a TV show. What a human tragedy! Any time we see young people being groomed to hate, we all have reasons to be gravely concerned about our nation's future.

It would have been well if the United States had continued the progress we were making in racial uplift based upon affirmative action. We could have been more prepared to embrace the many nonwhite immigrants who now dwell in our urban centers. Instead, this rapid upward mobility of blacks that had been made possible through such strategies as aggressive employment procedures, contract set-asides, and scholarships was aborted. Presidents have not exercised their moral influence in the right direction. The Supreme Court and the Justice Department have put law against racial justice. As a result we have created by our negligence and insensitivity a larger and growing black underclass that is a time bomb for all Americans, white as well as black. Many of these young people are completely outside of the American society, and they have developed their own culture of survival. Life for them is brutal and short. It is devoid of any sense of right or wrong. There is no respect for human life, including their own. These young people often have no knowledge of family, school, or church. They know only a human jungle in which one does what one has to do to survive. Often this means kill or be killed. Now that drugs have saturated these urban neighborhoods, young boys have become assassins for wealthy drug kingpins. Unless this situation is seen for what it is, we will see a further degeneration of not just black life but all life in this society. A cancer like this is bound to spread.

I shall call this inner-city underclass culture "rap culture." Rap is a form of music that has developed in this subculture. This music has a certain beat that appeals to young people who grow up in this type of social environment. On the male side, this culture is gratuitously violent; on the female side, it is manifested through the breeding of offspring. Having babies is celebrated as an indication that one belongs. And, in such a loveless culture, girls feel the need of someone to love. AIDS and crack babies add to the woeful outcome of an environment infested with drugs, poverty, and unbridled sex. Black pastors report that young people in these environments sometimes step forward to seek a different life. Whether these young people come on their own or are sought through the outreach of churches, they present a special challenge.

Black pastors indicate that these young people know little if anything about family life. They have no sense of right or wrong. They have never read the Bible or been to Sunday school. Boys, especially, know nothing about discipline. They do or say what they want at will. They are likely to be armed with a knife or gun. They have not known of such organizations as Boy Scouts or Girl Scouts. In other words, the usual experiences of middle-class Americans, black or white, are not theirs. On a panel recently, I was shocked as I discussed racism with a group of young adults from this type of environment. At twenty-five to thirty years of age, they had had no real contact with mainstream American society. They were so deeply involved in sex and drugs that they had no knowledge of what was going on in the rest of the world. As I tried to get them to see some of the problems in the macroculture, they frankly declared they did not care or understand what I was trying to say. For them life is "a useless passion." They live life "a day at a time." Life is like quicksand. Some are struggling to get out of a bottomless pit, but all the while their feet keep slipping. In such an instance one feels almost helpless to communicate. One needs mainly to listen. How can you have answers, when you do not understand the questions?

Confronted with this situation, it seemed to me that a more personal dimension of the Christian faith had to be expressed. Social analysis was bankrupt in this situation. The problem here was *meaning*. Fortunately, I had spent many years trying to understand existentialism in theological terms. The young men and women before me had a crisis of meaning. This question of meaning had to be addressed before they could begin to care or understand about the social, economic, and political concerns that I was prepared to discuss. It helped to tune in on their concerns. I found them to be very effective in describing their pain.

In this area of concern black theology has been inadequate. It has been one-dimensional in the direction of political concerns. This emphasis is both its strength and its weakness. It has been a powerful corrective to much of evangelical theology that has majored in personal faith. However, I do not think much evangelical theology has plumbed the depths of the proper existential analysis of faith. On the other hand, black theology has not for the most part majored in a serious concern for personal sin and salvation. It has not stressed the quest for meaning in personal life. It has not, as I discussed concerning the spirituals, lifted up the deep spiritual taproots of black religious experience. Thus it has not been as therapeutic as it should have been for those who need meaning and healing in their lives. This lacuna in black theology thus far is the result of a lack of attention to a powerful resource inherent in black religious experience and its African roots. A black theology with a focus on ministry must no longer neglect this existential dimension of black religious experience. It must be recovered and reinterpreted in light of the broader concerns of black theology.

Black theology at its best is holistic. It is also more authentic when it maintains a balance between its priestly and prophetic dimensions.

Again, it is existential as well as political. At the same time that it speaks to this-worldly social, economic, and political issues, it also addresses the human condition in terms of sin, guilt, and grace. Although these views are not recent ones in my own theological reflections, they need to be re-stated and updated for the present and the future.

African religious experience has always included the total self, body as well as mind. Thinking is not excluded, but willing and feeling are also embraced in religious worship. About two years ago, I worshiped with a colored congregation in Cape Town, South Africa. It was a rela-tively formal worship service. These were middle-class mixed people, rather than what in South Africa are designated as "black Africans." There was a surprise after the benediction. All the chairs were arranged around the wall. Religious music was played and the entire assembled body began a session of dancing. It was not a romantic dance between men and women but more of a spontaneous "holy dance" in which all persons present—men, women, and children—were participating. It was a sacred celebrative type of dancing in conclusion to the afternoon's activities. Responses to my many questions indicated that those who worshiped considered this as part of a celebrative religious event.

In townships like Soweto I had seen this bodily form of worship as part of the regular worship service. One of the things that puzzled me was the joyous nature of the hymns, prayers, and sermons. It was diffi-cult for me to understand how so much daily pain could be translated into such exalted praise in the presence of God. Upon second thought, it was no longer strange. I only needed to be reminded of the nature of black worship back home. A Nigerian student I met in Lagos later stud-ied at the Howard Divinity School. He once told me that there was, in his view, a similarity between the worship of black people in some of the storefront churches in Washington, D.C., and traditional religious wor-ship in African villages.

What is most important, I believe, is that religion claims the whole person, body and spirit. Thought is lived-thought. It is not a head trip, but neither is it without intellectual reflection. Holistic black worship re-quires that we bring our heads to church as well as our hearts. We are beings that think, but thinking is related to willing and feeling as well. The whole person is caught up in religious conviction and commitment. Only thus is black religious experience holistic. There needs to be teach-ing as well as preaching in our sermons and in the total life and witness of black churches. This constructive direction of the holism is authentic to the African American religious tradition.

The existential and the social (interpersonal) aspects of black religion are balanced in this holistic black religious expression. Human persons have a self-conscious, self-transcendence in them. We are not only conscious, we are also self-conscious. This means that we are capable of self-analysis. We need meaning, goals, values, and purpose. Self-respect, self-affirmation, and a sense of self-worth are essential to a healthy personality. At the same time we are persons in relation to other persons. Our nature is unfulfilled unless it reaches out to other persons in wholesome relationships. Sociability is built into human nature as it is given to us and discovered and known by us. Thus, wholesome friendships and family associations are essential to persons and persons-in-community. All of this and more we find in our African roots, which have been a part of authentic black religious traditions in the United States. A kinship system has sustained black people amid horrendous circumstances in the American environment. It is instructive that black churches were birthed by mutual aid societies based upon the kinship bonds of black people. These early societies often had "African" in their title. Thus, a black theology for ministry must be conscious of this kinship aspect to effective witness in and through black churches.[8]

Finally, the holistic black religious experience must encompass balance between the priestly and prophetic dimensions. I have written extensively about this priestly-prophetic merger in black religion and in the black church tradition.[9]

Black Church Theology and Ministry— An Unfinished Agenda

In the course of this study I have discovered many things that need further attention. The most sobering lesson is that no one person or volume can cover the agenda for the mission and ministry of black churches. As a theologian I am aware that there are limits to what I can contribute to any discussion on ministry. My role is more critical and reflective than empirical and practical. This role can be a helpful support for those who are too busy in the practice of ministry for the research and reflection that the theologian can bring to bear upon ministry. Throughout this study I have attempted to be a theologian with a pastor's heart. Even though it has been many years since I have been in the pastoral role, I still recall the years of my involvement. Furthermore, I have spent most of my three and more decades of academic work preparing men and women to minister in the church. Theological education has been my prime vocation even though I have sometimes served in a purely academic role as researcher, writer, teacher, and journalist.

In concluding this study, I will focus upon three aspects of an unfinished agenda: theological education, graduate programs in religious studies, and continuing education. In each case I will state the need as I see it and make direct recommendations.

Theological education for ministry in black churches deserves direct attention. As I have pointed out throughout this study, black churches have a specific assignment in ministry. Blacks did not choose to develop a subculture; it has developed out of oppression and the necessity to find a way to survive in a hostile environment. Religion and church have nurtured this survival culture. Even now black churches serve as nurturing communities for black people from all backgrounds and positions in life, including men and women in exalted corporate and government positions.

There are only three fully accredited black theological seminaries in the nation. It has been my privilege to serve in all three. For more than twenty-two years, I was professor of theology at the Howard University Divinity School. I was granted tenure early and served on the faculty senate for more than a decade. At Howard University, it was also my privilege to edit the *Journal of Religious Thought*. For one year, while on leave from Howard University, I was dean of the school of theology at Virginia Union University. From 1980 to 1983, I was president of the Interdenominational Theological Center, which is sponsored by six denominations and is perhaps the largest black theological center in the world. Presently I continue my work as a theologian at Eastern Baptist Theological Seminary. My experience in these institutions, as well as all of my academic and ministerial endeavors, provide the background for my concern about theological education and the preparation of effective, theologically educated leadership for black churches.

The education of ministers is so critical that this issue deserves a lengthy treatment. Only a small percentage of black church leaders are seminary educated. The majority of these leaders receive their education in predominantly white seminaries. Many of these seminaries are dominated by European scholarship. Decision making is usually in the hands of white males. This is true of faculty decisions as well as trustee deliberations. Administration and governance as well as subject matter pay inadequate attention to the black reality in American life. Black graduates are more qualified to minister to white suburban congregations than to their own people. Seminaries are generally "miseducating" black seminarians for ministry in black churches. The problem is less evident in black seminaries, but they, too, often lean away from immersion in the black experience to maintain accreditation in an enterprise where standards are set by white leaders.

Diversity in education is slow in coming to American seminary communities. Secular academic institutions are often driven by legal requirements to make substantive changes to correct past injustices. Seminaries, which follow the slow pace of denominational concerns, do not usually see diversity as important, especially insofar as knowledge and power are concerned. Much thought, attention, and action will be needed to bring racial equality and justice to the seminaries that provide education for so many black people who will be ministering in black churches for the rest of their lives. Obviously, I see theological education, even though flawed, as more desirable than its absence. Anyone with a well-trained mind has the possibility of adapting that knowledge to the needs and circumstances of their congregations. Nevertheless, more needs to be done to incorporate black experience and leadership into the theological education enterprise.

We also need to prepare more people for teaching and research in the field of religion. Only a few black religious scholars are currently on the faculties of colleges and universities. I am especially concerned about the need for men and women with Ph.D.'s to serve on seminary faculties and to staff denominational positions that require exceptional amounts of knowledge. For instance, these persons are needed to prepare educational literature for black churches. They are also needed to participate in the educational research and writing in predominantly white denominations. At present we are not even able to replenish the faculty vacancies in black seminaries and colleges.

The emergence of the doctor of ministry degree has been both a curse and a blessing for black ministers. The availability of the D.Min. has caused many blacks capable of earning the Ph.D. to opt for a shorter route to "doctor" status. Some counselors, who think that most blacks do not have the ability to earn the Ph.D., have counseled capable black students to settle for a D.Min. A decreasing number of black males are studying for the Ph.D. There has been an increase in candidates for the Ph.D. among black women, probably because ordination is not as readily available to black women. The D.Min. is useful for those persons who are certain that a professional ministry is where they will fulfill their vocation of ministry. It aids them in doing advanced study related to a particular skill or aspect of ministry where they desire to be most effective. There is a need for realistic counseling of prospective advanced students. They need to know exactly what these degrees involve. In other words, a decision this momentous should be an "informed" decision. One of the most tortured decisions I had to make as a seminary dean or president was to inform one of my own gifted students that a D.Min. did not qualify him for a particular faculty position.

A final general challenge has to do with the need for what I will call a think tank for information and action related to ministry in the black church. There is a need for a black church institute in most major cities in this country. The institute would be a place where important issues in the particular metropolitan area would be discussed. This setting would not replace the ministerial fellowships. It would be of a different order and serve a purpose now neglected. Ministerial fellowships are for the purpose of *fellowship* and the preaching event. Other concerns receive a superficial and passing attention. Often these ministerial groups converge around elections, but serious study, reflection, and research are not a part of their agenda. As a consequence, black ministers usually "follow the leader" when it comes to the support of political candidates or issues to be decided on behalf of black people.

A think tank would provide for research, study, and reflection on issues of great significance in an urban setting. Ministers would assemble the best-informed persons—scholars, researchers, activists, professionals, and others—to advise on major decisions. There would be the output of facts, data, information in workshops and conferences. These meetings would close with suggestions on tactics and strategies for action based upon the best knowledge available. The leadership would be clergy and lay and the audience would be equally mixed. Men, women, and young people would all struggle with the issues. Publications for study would be released.

What we have at present are think tanks made up of nonreligious and nonchurch persons. There is a tendency to exclude pastor-scholars and full-time religious scholars from these deliberations. Yet most decisions and decisive actions in the black community are based in black churches. Black ministers and churches come in for severe criticism for not acting in a responsible and informed way on key issues. The black church institute could be a means not only of responding to criticism but of providing for informed and responsible action for and by black churches on all kinds of issues. AIDS, sex education, homosexuality, homelessness, violence, criminal justice, drug abuse, and medical ethics (for example, regarding organ transplants) are some of these issues.

The black church institute should be funded by churches on an ecumenical basis. It should be staffed by a competent scholar-director, usually someone capable of quantifiable research. The director could be clergy or lay, man or woman. The director should be a church person with a passion for social justice. A theologian or other competent person capable of serious biblical and theological reflection should be associated with the institute. The institute should be closely related to institutions in the community that are in a position to share facilities, resources, and knowledge to enrich and empower its vital mission. For example, colleges, seminaries, universities, hospitals, penal institutions, and courts could be partners in this important effort. The institute would see its mission as a vital resource to ministry through the churches. Its board of directors and decision-making leadership should be in minority hands to assure that the mission of black churches will always be a priority on its agenda. It should be available, however, as a resource to all who seek racial justice and the humanization of life.

Summary

We have closed our discussion by focusing upon the faith and praxis of black churches. The direction is to the future. Several ideologies present in the black church and community are new and different. Inasmuch as black people are being informed and influenced by these ideologies, black religious leaders need to give serious thought to them. Some theological reflection upon the practice of ministry, with some concrete examples, was provided. Finally, an agenda for black church theology and for ministerial leadership was outlined. If this agenda and these recommendations are taken seriously, the multiple problems of the black community can be factually considered and ministry through black churches can become more effective. May the reader be set upon a quest for the knowledge and resources needed for a more responsible ministry in the church of Jesus Christ.

Notes

Introduction

1. J. Deotis Roberts, *Black Theology in Dialogue* (Philadelphia: Westminster Press, 1987), 18.
2. Gayraud S. Wilmore, *Black Religion and Black Radicalism* (New York: Doubleday & Co., 1972; 2d ed., Maryknoll, N.Y.: Orbis Books, 1983).
3. J. Deotis Roberts, *Roots of a Black Future* (Philadelphia: Westminster Press, 1980).

Chapter 1: Jesus, the Church, and Ministry

1. *The Interpreter's Bible*, vol. VIII (Nashville: Abingdon Press, 1952), on Luke 4:18.
2. Paul Tillich, *The Courage to Be* (New Haven, Conn.: Yale University Press, 1953).
3. Martin Luther King, Jr., *Stride Toward Freedom* (San Francisco: Harper & Row, 1986), 90–107.
4. Howard Thurman, *Jesus and the Disinherited* (Richmond, Ind.: Friends United Press, 1981).
5. John S. Mbiti, *African Religions and Philosophies* (Garden City, N.Y.: Doubleday & Co., Anchor Books, 1970), 31–32.
6. Sallie McFague, *Metaphorical Theology: Models of God in Religious Language* (Philadelphia: Fortress Press, 1982), 15.
7. Susan Brooks Thistlethwaite, *Metaphors for the Contemporary Church* (New York: Pilgrim Press, 1983), 10.
8. Paul Minear, *Images of the Church in the New Testament* (Philadelphia: Westminster Press, 1960).
9. Avery Dulles, *Models of the Church* (Garden City, N.Y.: Doubleday & Co., 1974).

Chapter 2: Ministry in the Black Tradition

1. The work by Carter G. Woodson titled *The History of the Negro Church* (Washington, D.C.: Associated Publishers, 1921) is a classic study that is foundational and has gone into several editions.
2. Gayraud S. Wilmore, *Black Religion and Black Radicalism*, 2d ed. (Maryknoll, N.Y.: Orbis Books, 1983). The work was first published by Doubleday in 1972. As historian of the black church/theology movement, Wilmore has done much to set the record straight regarding the important role of black church leaders in the black freedom struggle.
3. James Henry Harris, "Preaching Liberation in the Black Church," *Christian Century* (June 13–20, 1990), 599.
4. Ibid.
5. Ibid., 599–600.
6. Ibid., 602.
7. Wilmore, "Connecting Two Worlds" (a response to James Henry Harris), *Christian Century* (June 13–20, 1990), 601.
8. Ibid.
9. Peter J. Paris, *The Social Teaching of the Black Churches* (Philadelphia: Fortress Press, 1985), 3–4.
10. Ibid., 6.
11. Ibid.
12. Wilmore, *Black Religion and Black Radicalism*. See also C. Eric Lincoln and Lawrence H. Mamiya, *The Black Church in the African American Experience* (Durham, N.C.: Duke University Press, 1990).
13. J. Deotis Roberts, "Ecumenical Concerns Among National Baptists," *Journal of Ecumenical Studies* 17, no. 2 (1980).
14. James M. Washington, *The Frustrated Fellowship of Black Baptists* (Macon, Ga.: Mercer University Press, 1986).
15. James H. Cone, *For My People* (Maryknoll, N.Y.: Orbis Books, 1984).
16. William Julius Wilson, *The Truly Disadvantaged: The Inner City, the Underclass, and Public Policy* (Chicago: University of Chicago Press, 1987).
17. W. J. Wilson, *The Declining Significance of Race*, 2d ed. (Chicago: University of Chicago Press, 1980).
18. See Wilson, *Truly Disadvantaged*, vii, 6–14.
19. Ibid., 12.
20. Ibid., 21–29.

Chapter 3: The Prophethood of Black Believers

1. Gayraud S. Wilmore, *Black Religion and Black Radicalism* (Philadelphia: Westminster Press, 1987). See also J. H. Cone, *Black Theology and*

Black Power (Maryknoll, N.Y.: Orbis Books, 1968), and Joseph Washington, *Black Religion* (Boston: Beacon Press, 1964).

2. J. Deotis Roberts, *A Black Political Theology* (Philadelphia: Westminster Press, 1974), 204. The term "African American" will be used interchangeably with "black" until further definition occurs.

3. Because of their association with the Bush Administration, they are known as Black Neo-Conservatives.

4. Abraham Cohen, *Everyman's Talmud* (New York: Schocken Books, 1975), xvi.

5. Several sources speak specially to this topic, including: Bruce Hilton, *The Delta Ministry* (London: Collier Macmillian, 1969); Pat Hoffman, *Ministry of the Dispossessed: Learning from the Farm Workers Movement* (Los Angeles: Wallace Press, 1987); Charles F. Kemp, *Pastoral Care with the Poor* (Nashville: Abingdon Press, 1972).

6. See C. Eric Lincoln and L. H. Mamiya, *The Black Church in the African American Experience* (Durham, N.C.: Duke University Press, 1990), ch. 7. Here Lincoln studies and reports on the black church and black consciousness. His study validates much that I have indicated regarding the profound meaning of *blackness*.

7. *The State of Black America 1991*, ed. Janet Dewart (New York: National Urban League, 1991), 4.

8. Ibid., 26. See also pp. 25–27.

9. Ibid., 211–12. A series of recommendations are set forth regarding race relations, federal budget, economic development, employment, civil rights, education, crime and criminal justice, health, housing, energy, and international affairs. African Americans could profit by the implementation of all these recommendations. See pp. 213–16. See also Lincoln, *The Black Church in the African American Experience*, chs. 8 and 9.

10. The Martin Luther King Jr. Fellows are now senior scholar-pastors in outstanding pastorates nationwide. They were selected as fellows at Colgate-Rochester Divinity School when Professor Henry Mitchell was Dean of Black Church Studies. The project focused upon young, gifted pastors who had a professional theological degree. They went on to earn a D.Min. degree in order to return to parish work. Most published their studies and have been unusually effective in ministry.

11. Here I recommend two additional sources that the reader will find extremely useful: David Claerbaut, *Urban Ministry* (Grand Rapids: Zondervan Publishing House, 1983); James H. Harris, *Black Ministers and Laity in the Urban Church* (Lanham, Md.: University Press of America, 1987).

Chapter 4: Education as Ministry

1. Grant S. Shockley, "Black Pastoral Leadership in Religious Education: Social Justice Correlates," in *The Pastor as Religious Educator*, ed. Robert L. Browning (Birmingham, Ala.: Religious Education Press), 206.
2. See Lawrence Kohlberg, "Moral and Religious Education and the Public Schools," in *Religion and Public Education*, ed. Theodore R. Sizer (New York: Houghton Mifflin Co., 1967), 165–82.
3. See F. Clark Power et al., *Kohlberg's Approach to Moral Education* (New York: Columbia University Press, 1989). See especially the essay by Moshe Blatt (11–32).
4. Kohlberg is representative of a group of kindred thinkers who have much interest in education and human development, thinkers such as Jean Piaget, John Dewey, Erik Erikson, and Emile Durkheim. All are social scientists, except Dewey. Therefore, a strong component of experimentation is inherent in their work.
5. Avery Dulles, "Religion," *Washington Post*, Oct. 24, 1992, B7.

Chapter 5: Faith Development and Ministry to Black Youth

1. James Fowler, *Faith Development* (Philadelphia: Fortress Press, 1987).
2. See *The State of America's Children* (Washington, D.C.: Children's Defense Fund, 1992), 2.
3. C. Eric Lincoln and L. H. Mamiya, *The Black Church in the African American Experience* (Durham, N.C.: Duke University Press, 1990), 322.
4. Ibid., 326.
5. Ibid., 332.
6. An increasing number of studies treat the plight of the underclass, a high percentage of which is constituted by black youth. See Ken Auletta, *The Underclass* (New York: Random House, 1982). This comprehensive study includes a good bibliography.

Chapter 6: The Black Minister and Pastoral Care

1. More detailed information on my approach to the "priestly" and "prophetic" dimensions and how they interface in a "holistic" gospel will be found in my *Liberation and Reconciliation* (Philadelphia: Westminster Press, 1972) and *A Black Political Theology* (Philadelphia: Westminster Press, 1974).
2. Edward P. Wimberly, *Pastoral Care in the Black Church* (Nashville: Abingdon Press, 1979). While I was president of the Interdenominational

Theological Center, Wimberly was on the faculty. I learned to appreciate much of Wimberly's contribution to this field during our personal friendship and dialogue. There has been much give-and-take between the Wimberlys (Edward and his wife, Anne) and myself.

3. (Nashville: Abingdon Press, 1991). Wimberly has continued to be a productive writer, and I will touch upon several of his works.

4. Ibid., 9–10.

5. Harold A. Carter, Wyatt Tee Walker, and William A. Jones, Jr., *The Black Church Looks at the Bicentennial* (Elgin, Ill.: Progressive National Baptist Publishing House, 1976), 83.

6. Calvin B. Marshall III, "The Black Church—Its Mission Is Liberation," in *The Black Experience in Religion*, ed. C. Eric Lincoln (New York: Doubleday & Co., Anchor Books, 1977), 162.

7. Ibid., 164.

8. David Hurst, *The Shepherding of Black Christians*, Th.D. diss. (Ann Arbor, Mich.: University Microfilms, 1981), 273.

9. Wayne E. Oates, *Pastoral Counseling in Social Problems* (Grand Rapids: Baker Book House, 1965). Quoted by Hurst in *Shepherding of Black Christians*, 273.

Chapter 7: Black Women and Ministry

1. C. Eric Lincoln and Lawrence H. Mamiya, *The Black Church in the African American Experience* (Durham, N.C.: Duke University Press, 1990), ch. 10.

2. Robert E. Hood, *Must God Remain Greek?* (Minneapolis: Fortress Press, 1990).

3. Many other passages in scripture are used to support sexism in general and in the ministry in particular. See Cain Felder, *Troubling Biblical Waters* (Maryknoll, N.Y.: Orbis Books, 1989), 139–49.

4. Carl Marbury was part of a discussion group made up of black women and men at the Ecumenical and Cultural Research Institute, Collegeville, Minn. The group was co-chaired by Thomas Hoyt and me, and we met for three summer sessions. A comprehensive account, together with my personal reflections, is in *The A.M.E. Zion Quarterly Review*, 99, no. 3 (October 1988): 20–29. My article is titled: "The Quest for Mutuality: Confronting Sexism in the Black Church."

5. Jacquelyn Grant, *White Women's Christ and Black Women's Jesus* (Decatur, Ga.: Scholars Press, 1989).

6. Katie G. Cannon, *Black Womanist Ethics* (Decatur, Ga.: Scholars Press, 1988).

7. See, for example, Ella Mitchell, *Those Preachin' Black Women*, 2 vols. (Valley Forge, Pa.: Judson Press, 1985–88).

8. The following are just a few black women's literary productions in theology and church studies: in addition to the Grant and Cannon works listed above, see Janice E. Hale, *Black Children* (Baltimore: Johns Hopkins, 1986); Suzan Johnson, ed., *Wise Women Bearing Gifts* (Valley Forge, Pa.: Judson Press, 1990); and Renita J. Weems, *Just a Sister Away* (San Diego, Calif.: Lura Media, 1988). Much creative work exists in articles and essays, and several black women are currently at work on book-length essays.

9. James H. Cone, *A Black Theology of Liberation*, 2d ed. (Maryknoll, N.Y.: Orbis Books, 1986). Preface to 1986 edition, xvii–xviii.

10. See Cain Hope Felder, ed., *Stony the Road We Trod* (Minneapolis: Fortress Press, 1991).

Chapter 8: The Black Church and Economics

1. See J. Deotis Roberts, *Black Theology in Dialogue* (Philadelphia: Westminster Press, 1987), 82.

2. Ibid., 65–83.

3. Thomas W. Ogletree, *The Use of the Bible in Christian Ethics* (Philadelphia: Fortress Press, 1983).

4. See James Woodward, ed., *Embracing the Chaos* (London: SPCK, 1990). Quotation is from the foreword by Richard Oxon.

5. Cornel West, *Prophesy Deliverance!* (Philadelphia: Westminster Press, 1982), ch. 4.

6. Roberts, *Black Theology in Dialogue*, 39–41.

7. C. Eric Lincoln and Lawrence H. Mamiya, *The Black Church in the African American Experience* (Durham, N.C.: Duke University Press, 1990), 10–19, 240–44.

8. Ibid., 240–41.

9. Ibid.

10. Ibid., 242. See also 243–44.

11. Ibid., 245–46.

12. Ibid., 247–50.

13. W. E. B Du Bois, *The Philadelphia Negro* (New York: Schocken Books, 1970), 207.

14. I have presented my views more completely elsewhere. See "A Christian Perspective on the Economic Order," in *Human Rights: Christians, Marxists, and Others in Dialogue*, ed. Leonard Swidler (New York: Paragon House, 1991), 252–55.

15. Ibid., 257–58.

16. See, for example, Janet Dewart, ed., *The State of Black America 1991* (New York: National Urban League, 1991).

17. See J. Deotis Roberts, *Roots of a Black Future* (Philadelphia: Westminster Press, 1980).

18. Although Clarence Thomas was appointed to the Supreme Court to succeed Thurgood Marshall, a strong civil rights advocate, Thomas typifies in his statements as well as in his life the black person who denies the value of the affirmative action that helped him (or her) achieve success in the majority culture.

19. Floyd Dicksons, Jr., and Jacqueline Dickens, *The Black Manager* (New York: Macmillan Publishing Co., 1978).

20. D. Parke Gibson, *$70 Billion in the Black* (New York: Macmillan Publishing Co., 1978). In chapter 5 I mentioned the work of Leon Sullivan toward economic uplift. Sullivan considers his economic leadership as a vital part of his comprehensive ministry. See also J. Deotis Roberts, *Theological Commentary on the Sullivan Principles* (Philadelphia: I.C.E.O.P., 1980).

Chapter 9: The Black Church and Politics

1. In 1962 I wrote what appeared to me to be a proper foundation for the understanding of the state in the history of theology and ethics in the West. However, I did not at that time have the important contribution of Dr. M. L. King Jr., before me, nor the tremendous reflections coming out of the civil rights and black power movements. See J. Deotis Roberts, "Theological Conception of the State," *A Journal of Church and State*, 4, no. 1 (1962): 66–75.

2. See Albert Knudson, *The Principles of Christian Ethics* (New York: Abingdon-Cokesbury Press, 1943), 217–18.

3. Martin Luther King Jr., *Where Do We Go from Here: Chaos or Community?* (New York: Harper & Row, 1967).

4. C. Eric Lincoln and L. H. Mamiya, *The Black Church in the African American Experience* (Durham, N.C.: Duke University Press, 1990), ch. 1.

5. James H. Cone, *Martin and Malcolm and America: A Dream or a Nightmare* (Maryknoll, N.Y.: Orbis Books, 1991), 3–17.

6. Donald E. Messer, *Christian Ethics and Political Action* (Valley Forge, Pa.: Judson Press, 1984), ch. 1.

7. Waldo Beach, *Christian Ethics in the Protestant Tradition* (Atlanta: John Knox Press, 1988), 111.

8. Messer, *Christian Ethics and Political Action*, 39–40.

9. Ibid., 41.

10. See Sterling Stuckey, *The Ideological Origins of Black Nationalism* (Boston: Beacon Press, 1972).

11. Cone, *Martin and Malcolm and America*, 4.
12. Lincoln and Mamiya, *Black Church in the African American Experience*, 14–15. Here he writes about "resistance" and "accommodation."
13. Roger D. Hatch, *Beyond Opportunity* (Philadelphia: Fortress Press, 1988), 3. See Sheila D. Collins, *The Rainbow Challenge* (New York: Monthly Review Press, 1986).
14. James Melvin Washington, "Jesse Jackson and the Symbolic Politics of Black Christendom," *Annals of the American Academy of Political and Social Science* 480 (July 1985): 89–105.
15. See J. Deotis Roberts, *Black Theology Today* (Toronto: Edwin Mellen, 1982), 163.
16. Recent conversation with Wilson Goode, former mayor of Philadelphia, has been very instructive. Goode, a black Baptist deacon, has outlined the relationship he sees between faith and politics in his *In Goode Faith*, assisted by Joann Stevens (Valley Forge, Pa.: Judson Press, 1992).
17. A fuller account of my views is in *Black Theology in Dialogue* (Atlanta: Westminster Press, 1987), chs. 6–8.

Chapter 10: The Music Ministry in Black Churches

1. See Jon Michael Spencer, *Protest and Praise: Sacred Music of Black Religion* (Minneapolis: Fortress Press, 1990), viii. See also Geoffrey Wainwright, *Doxology: The Praise of God in Worship, Doctrine, and Life* (New York: Oxford University Press, 1980).
2. Ashenafi Kebede, *Roots of Black Music* (Englewood Cliffs, N.J.: Prentice-Hall, 1982), 93–95.
3. Ibid., 129.
4. Ibid. While his interpretation of music may be trustworthy, I would raise serious objections to what he has to say about religion, primarily in regard to his generalization regarding West African religion as "polytheistic" as compared to European religion as "monotheistic."
5. Ibid., 131.
6. See Harold Courlander, *Negro Folk Music, USA* (New York: Columbia University Press, 1963), 80–90.
7. Kebede, *Roots of Black Music*, 130.
8. Ibid., 131.
9. LeRoi Jones, *Blues People: Negro Music in White America* (New York: William Morrow & Co., 1963), 7.
10. Ibid., 17.
11. Phyl Garland, *The Sound of Soul* (New York: Henry Regnery, 1971), 40.
12. Ibid., 17.

13. Melville J. Herskovits, *The Myth of the Negro Past* (New York: Harper & Row, 1941), 265.
14. Garland, *Sound of Soul*, 43.
15. Ibid., 44.
16. Ibid., 44.
17. Wyatt Tee Walker, *Somebody's Calling My Name: Black Sacred Music and Social Change* (Valley Forge, Pa.: Judson Press, 1982), 22.
18. Ibid., 26.
19. The Howard Thurman Collection in the archives of the Medger Library at Boston University is a valuable resource for anyone seeking further information.
20. Howard Thurman, *Deep River and the Negro Spiritual Speaks of Life and Death* (Richmond, Ind.: Friends United Press, 1975), 60.
21. Ibid., 61.
22. Ibid., 63–64.
23. Ibid. See also "The Amazing Power of Music," in the *Bulletin* of the American Association of Retired Persons (February 1992), 13, 20, in which Dr. Oliver Sacks, a neurologist, writes about the therapeutic power of music.
24. James H. Cone, *Spirituals and Blues* (New York: Seabury Press, 1972).
25. Miles Mark Fisher, *Negro Slave Songs in the United States* (New York: Russell & Russell, 1968). See Bernard Katz, ed., *The Social Implications of Early Negro Music in the United States* (New York: Arno Press and the *New York Times*, 1969), 14.
26. See note 1 of this chapter.
27. See Cone, *Spirituals and Blues*.
28. Cecil Cone, *Identity-Crisis in Black Theology* (Nashville: AMEC, 1975), 63.
29. Spencer, *Protest and Praise*, ch. 9.
30. H. Richard Niebuhr, *Christ and Culture* (San Francisco: Harper & Row, 1951).
31. Louis Charles Harvey, "Black Gospel Music and Black Theology," *Journal of Religious Thought*, 43, no. 2 (Fall-Winter 1986–87): 27.
32. Spencer, *Protest and Praise*, 218.
33. See ibid., 218 n. 49.
34. Ibid., 202–3.
35. Henry H. Mitchell and Nicholas Cooper-Lewter, *Soul Theology: The Heart of American Black Culture* (San Francisco: Harper & Row, 1986), 95.
36. Spencer, *Protest and Praise*, 222.

Chapter 11: Faith and Praxis: What About the Future?

1. Alvin Toffler, *Power Shift* (New York: Bantam Books, 1991), 4.
2. Ibid., 7.

3. James H. Cone, *Martin and Malcolm and America: A Dream or a Nightmare* (Maryknoll, N.Y.: Orbis Books, 1991).
4. For example, see the February 1992 issue of *Ebony*, p. 110.
5. See Charlotte Allen, "Gray Matter, Black-and-White Controversy," *Insight* (January 5, 1992), 4–9.
6. Mervyn Farroe, "An Interview with Molefi Kete Asante," *Black Excellence* (November-December 1991), 56.
7. Ibid., 56–57.
8. See J. Deotis Roberts, *Roots of a Black Future* (Philadelphia: Westminster Press, 1988).
9. See J. Deotis Roberts, *Black Theology Today* (Toronto: Edwin Mellen, 1982), 179–87.

Index

Printed in the United States
1234600005BA/49-51